Not-for-Profit Financial Reporting: Mastering the Unique Requirements

By Bruce W. Chase, Ph.D., CPA

T0338195

Notice to readers

Not-for-Profit Financial Reporting: Mastering the Unique Requirements is intended solely for use in continuing professional education and not as a reference. It does not represent an official position of the American Institute of Certified Public Accountants, and it is distributed with the understanding that the author and publisher are not rendering legal, accounting, or other professional services in the publication. This course is intended to be an overview of the topics discussed within, and the author has made every attempt to verify the completeness and accuracy of the information herein. However, neither the author nor publisher can guarantee the applicability of the information found herein. If legal advice or other expert assistance is required, the services of a competent professional should be sought.

You can qualify to earn free CPE through our pilot testing program.
If interested, please visit https://aicpacompliance.polldaddy.com/s/pilot-testing-survey.

ISBN 978-1-119-74409-2 (paper)
ISBN 978-1-119-74412-2 (ePDF)
ISBN 978-1-119-74410-8 (ePub)
ISBN 978-1-119-74413-9 (obk)

Course Code: **746492**
NFPF GS-0419-0A
Revised: **February 2019**

V10018985_061020

Table of Contents

Chapter 1

Financial Reporting

Learning objectives

- Identify the two classes of net assets.

- Identify the basic financial statements prepared by not-for-profits (NFPs).

- Identify various reporting formats used by NFPs.

- Identify reporting issues related to investments and endowments.

Introduction

This chapter will discuss what basic information NFP entities must report in their financial statements. We will also discuss some of the reporting formats used by NFP entities.

FASB Accounting Standards Update (ASU) No. 2016-14, *Presentation of Financial Statements of Not-for-Profit Entities*, was released on August 18, 2016. This ASU changes the way all NFPs classify net assets and prepare financial statements. The standard is effective for annual financial statements issued for fiscal years beginning after December 15, 2017, and for interim periods within fiscal years beginning after December 15, 2018. Early application is permitted.

This chapter will cover the major accounting and financial reporting requirements under ASU No. 2016-14.

Net assets

Is there a difference between a class of net assets and a fund? Yes! A fund has a self-balancing set of accounts with assets, liabilities, and fund balance accounts, whereas net assets simply represent the difference between assets and liabilities.

How an entity maintains its internal records is not an issue addressed by FASB. Instead, FASB *Accounting Standards Codification* (ASC) 958, *Not-for-Profit Entities*, requires that information about each class of net assets be reported in the financial statements.

NFP organizations are unique in that they often receive substantial amounts of contributions. These donations can contain donor-imposed restrictions as to their use. Information about restrictions on net resources is important to financial statement users.

A donor-imposed restriction is defined as a stipulation (donors include other types of contributors, including makers of certain grants) that is more specific than the broad limits resulting from the nature of the organization, the environment in which it operates, and the purpose specified in its articles of incorporation or bylaws.

Net assets can be broken down into two classes[1] based on the existence or absence of donor-imposed restrictions as shown in exhibit 1-1.

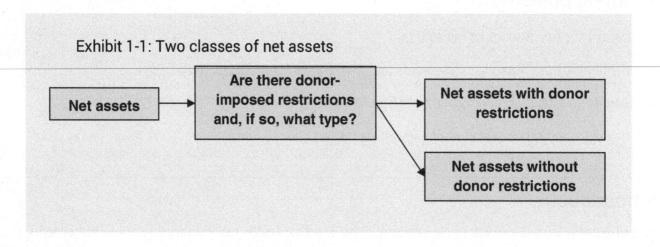

Exhibit 1-1: Two classes of net assets

The two classes of net assets are described as follows:

- *Net assets with donor restrictions*. The part of the net assets of an NFP that is subject to donor-imposed restrictions. These types of restrictions can be either temporary or perpetual in nature.
- *Net assets without donor restrictions*. The part of the net assets of an NFP that is not subject to donor-imposed restrictions.

[1] Prior to ASU No. 2016-14 there were three net asset classes (unrestricted, temporarily restricted, and permanently restricted). For more information, see the discussion following this section and fasb.org.

Footnote disclosures are required to include the timing and nature of the donor-imposed restrictions, as well as the composition of net assets with donor restrictions at the end of the period. The disclosures will continue to show an analysis by time, purpose, and perpetual restrictions.

At times, an NFP's governing board may make designations or appropriations that result in self-imposed limits on the use of resources without donor restrictions, known as board-designated net assets. FASB added a new requirement to disclose board designations on net assets without donor restrictions. Board-designated net assets can be described in the notes to the financial statements if the nature of the designation (that is, amount and purpose) is not clear from the description on the face of the statement of financial position.

> All net assets are classified as net assets without donor restrictions, unless the net assets result from contributions whose use is limited by donor-imposed stipulations.

Knowledge check

1. Which is accurate of net assets?

    a. Donor stipulations that are temporary or perpetual in nature will be footnote disclosed.
    b. Board-designated resources are reported as net assets with donor restrictions.
    c. In the absence of donor-imposed restrictions, net assets must be classified as net assets with donor restrictions.
    d. Endowment funds are classified as net assets with donor restrictions whose use is limited by donor-imposed stipulations that expire by passage of time.

The basic financial statements

FASB ASC 958 requires NFP entities to present financial statements showing aggregate information about the entity. It establishes minimum standards for financial reporting that are generally no more stringent than requirements for a business enterprise. In general, it allows significant flexibility in presenting certain information, allowing financial reporting to evolve to meet the needs of different NFP groups.

> The general purpose financial statements required by FASB ASC 958-205-05 for NFP entities are the statement of financial position, the statement of activities, the statement of cash flows, and accompanying notes to the financial statements. NFP entities must also present an analysis of expenses by function and nature in one location. This may be presented in the notes to the financial statements, in the statement of activities or as a separate statement. A fourth statement of functional expenses is no longer required only for certain NFP entities; this information must now be reported by all NFPs.

Other terms can be used for these statements, such as "balance sheet" for the statement of financial position. However, a statement of cash flows should only be titled as such.

Knowledge check

2. What is accurate of FASB ASC 958?

    a. In general, FASB ASC 958 allows no flexibility in presenting certain information.
    b. FASB ASC 958 focuses on reporting aggregated information about the entity as a whole.
    c. The general purpose financial statements required by FASB ASC 958 for NFP entities are the statement of financial position, the statement of activities, the statement of cash flows, the statement of functional expense and accompanying notes to the financial statements.
    d. FASB ASC 958 changed the requirement to report information about funds.

The statement of financial position

A statement of financial position reports an entity's assets, liabilities, and net assets. Generally, assets and liabilities should be aggregated into reasonably homogeneous groups. Assets need not be disaggregated on the basis of the presence of donor-imposed restrictions on their use; for example, cash available for current use without donor restrictions need not be reported separately from cash received with donor-imposed restrictions that is also available for current use. However, cash or other assets either (a) designated for long-term purposes or (b) received with donor-imposed restrictions that limit their use to long-term purposes should not be aggregated on a statement of financial position with cash or other assets that is available for current use. For example, cash that has been received with donor-imposed restrictions limiting its use to the acquisition of long-lived assets should be reported under a separate caption, such as "cash restricted to investment in property and equipment," and displayed near the section of the statement where property and equipment is displayed. The kind of asset should be described in the notes to the financial statements if its nature is not clear from the description on the face of the statement of financial position.

As illustrated in the following, assets and liabilities can be presented in a number of ways to provide information about liquidity.

Approaches to providing information about liquidity

- Sequencing assets according to their nearness of conversion to cash and sequencing liabilities according to the nearness of their maturity and resulting use of cash.
- Classifying assets and liabilities as current and noncurrent, as defined by FASB ASC 210-10.
- Disclosing in notes to financial statements any additional relevant information about the liquidity or maturity of assets and liabilities, including restrictions on the use of particular assets.

ASU No. 2016-14 includes disclosure requirements aimed at improving a financial statement user's understanding of an entity's liquidity and how it is being managed. NFPs are required to disclose the following quantitative and qualitative information about liquidity of assets and short-term demands on those assets:

- Qualitative information on how an NFP manages its liquid resources available to meet cash needs for general expenditures within one year of the balance sheet date
- Quantitative information that communicates the availability of financial assets at the balance sheet date to meet cash needs for general expenditures within one year of the balance sheet date

The statement of financial position should focus on the entity as a whole. It does this by reporting total assets, total liabilities, and total net assets for the entity. In addition, the amount of each of the two classes of net assets must also be reported.

Information about the nature and amounts of different types of restrictions on net assets with donor restrictions should be either reported on the face of the statement or in the notes to the financial statement. Separate lines in the statement may be used for purpose, time, and perpetual restrictions, such as support of a particular operating activity, investment for a specified term, or use in a specified period.

At times, an NFP's governing board may make designations or appropriations that result in self-imposed limits on the use of resources without donor restrictions, known as board-designated net assets. Information about the nature and amounts of different types of designation or appropriation on net assets without donor restrictions should be either reported on the face of the statement or in the notes to the financial statement.

In cases where separate lines are used in any of the two classes of net assets, a total must still be reported for each of the two classes of net assets.

Exhibit 1-2 reports one example of a statement of financial position after the implementation of ASU No. 2016-14. Note that this example sequences assets and liabilities based on liquidity and does not display information about the nature of restrictions on the face of the financial statement.

Exhibit 1-2

Not-for-profit "A"
Statement of Financial Position
December 31, 20X8 and 20X7
(in thousands)

	20X8	20X7
Assets:		
Cash and cash equivalents	$ 85	$ 560
Accounts and interest receivable	1,130	1,680
Inventories and prepaid expenses	710	1,020
Contributions receivable	3,025	2,700
Short-term investments	6,410	5,560
Collections of works of art (Note X)	-	-
Land, buildings, and equipment	60,600	63,580
Long-term investments	218,070	203,500
Total assets	$290,030	$278,600

Exhibit 1-2 (continued)

Not-for-profit "A"
Statement of Financial Position
December 31, 20X8 and 20X7
(in thousands)

	20X8	20X7
Liabilities and net assets:		
Accounts payable	$ 2,070	$ 1,150
Refundable advance	200	450
Grants payable	675	1,500
Notes payable	500	1,040
Long-term debt	7,185	8,200
Total liabilities	10,630	12,340
Net assets:		
Without donor restrictions	113,138	103,770
With donor restrictions	166,262	162,490
Total net assets	279,400	266,260
Total liabilities and net assets	$290,030	$278,600

The statement of activities

In many ways, the statement of activities is like an income statement for an NFP entity. However, because NFP entities have an operating purpose other than making a profit, terms like income statement and net income are not used. Instead, the terms "statement of activities" and "change in net assets" are used.

The statement of activities focuses on the entity as a whole and requires that the amount of change in net assets for the period be reported. In addition, the amount of change in net assets without donor restrictions and net assets with donor restrictions must also be reported.

The statement of activities reports revenues, gains, expenses, and losses for the period. Revenues are reported as increases in net assets without donor restrictions unless the use of the assets received is limited by donor-imposed restrictions. Likewise, gains and losses recognized on investments and other assets (or liabilities) are reported as increases or decreases in net assets without donor restrictions unless their use is restricted by explicit donor stipulations or by law.

In the statement of activities...

All expenses are reported as decreases in net assets without donor restrictions. That may seem somewhat odd at first. However, as entities use resources to meet donor-restricted purposes, the resources are released from restrictions and the expenses are reported as a decrease in net assets without donor restrictions.

An entity must report information about the nature and functional classification of expenses, such as major classes of program services and supporting activities. This information can be done on the face of the statement of activities, as a separate statement, or in the notes to the financial statements. Therefore, entities can display expenses either by natural or functional classification in the statement of activities as long as the functional information is presented.

Events that simultaneously increase one class of net assets and decrease another class of net assets (reclassifications) are reported as separate items in the statement of activities. For example, using resources to meet a donor-stipulated purpose restriction would simultaneously decrease net assets with donor restrictions and increase net assets without donor restrictions.

NFP entities have a great deal of flexibility in how items are sequenced in the statement of activities. Revenues, gains, expenses, losses, and reclassifications can be arranged in a variety of orders. In addition, an entity may choose to report some intermediate measure of operations, such as operating revenues over expenses.

Exhibit 1-2 reports one example of a statement of activities after implementation of ASU No. 2016-14. Note that this example uses three columns to display information: two for the classes of net assets and one total column. Also, note that change in total net assets as well as changes in the two classes of net assets is reported. Reclassifications (net assets released from restrictions) are reported separately.

Exhibit 1-2

Not-for-profit "B"
Statement of Activities
Year ended December 31, 20X8
(in thousands)

	Net Assets without Donor Restrictions	Net Assets with Donor Restrictions	Total
Revenues, gains, and other support:			
Contributions	$ 8,790	$ 9,480	$ 18,270
Fees	5,600		5,600
Income on long-term investments (Note F)	5,200	1,710	6,910
Other investment income (Note F)	650		650
Net unrealized and realized gains on long-term investments (Note F)	8,628	7,472	16,100
Net assets released from restrictions (Note E):			
Satisfaction of program restrictions	13,490	(13,490)	
Expiration of time restrictions	1,250	(1,250)	
Total revenues, gains, and other support	43,608	3,922	47,530
Expenses:			
Program 1	12,380		12,380
Program 2	9,340		9,340
Program 3	2,720		2,720
Management and general	5,460		5,460
Fund-raising	4,150		4,150
Total expenses (Note G)	34,050		34,050
Change in net assets	9,558	3,922	13,480
Net assets at beginning of year	120,675	183,470	304,145
Net assets at end of year	$130,233	$187,392	$ 317,625

Knowledge check

3. Which is accurate regarding the statement of activities?

    a. In many ways, the statement of activities is like an income statement for an NFP entity.
    b. Because NFP entities have an operating purpose other than making a profit, terms like income statement and net income are used.
    c. The statement of activities focuses on segments of the entity.
    d. An entity must report some intermediate measure of operations, such as operating revenues over expenses.

4. Which is accurate regarding the statement of activities?

    a. The statement of activities reports revenues, gains, expenses, and losses for the period.
    b. Revenues are reported as increases in net assets with donor restrictions unless the use of the assets received is limited by donor-imposed restrictions.
    c. All expenses are reported as decreases in net assets with donor restrictions.
    d. NFP entities have little flexibility in how items are sequenced in the statement of activities.

The statement of cash flows

FASB ASC 958-205-05-5 requires NFP entities to report a statement of cash flows. Entities should follow the provisions of FASB ASC 230-10-45.

> The listing of financing activities in FASB ASC 230-10-45-14 includes cash receipts that are donor-restricted for long-term purposes. Some examples would be contributions for capital assets and additions to an endowment. However, because cash restricted for long-term purposes is normally excluded from cash available for current use, a cash contribution for a long-term purpose would normally be reported as both a cash inflow from financing activities and a cash outflow from investing activities.

Entities may report cash flows from operating activities using either the direct or indirect method. If the direct method is used, ASU No. 2016-14 removes the requirement to present the indirect method reconciliation.

For business enterprises, net income is used as the starting point in the indirect method and the reconciliation required under the direct method. For NFP entities, change in total net assets should be used. In addition, cash flow from operating activities would include, if applicable, agency transactions. Exhibit 1-3 presents an example statement of cash flows using the indirect method.

Exhibit 1-3

Not-for-Profit "C"
Statement of Cash Flows
Year Ended December 31, 20X8
(in thousands)

Cash flows from operating activities:	
Change in net assets	$ 15,500
Adjustments to reconcile change in net assets to net cash used by operating activities:	
Depreciation	4,000
Increase in accounts and interest receivable	(640)
Decrease in inventories and prepaid expenses	290
Increase in contributions receivable	(425)
Increase in accounts payable	2,520
Decrease in refundable advance	(450)
Decrease in grants payable	(400)
Contributions restricted for long-term investment	(3,540)
Interest and dividends restricted for long-term investment	(400)
Net unrealized and realized gains on long-term investments	(16,800)
Net cash used by operating activities	(345)
Cash flows from investing activities:	
Purchase of equipment	(1,500)
Proceeds from sale of investments	70,000
Purchase of investments	(78,200)
Net cash used by investing activities	(9,700)
Cash flows from financing activities:	
Proceeds from contributions restricted for:	
Investment in endowment	300

Exhibit 1-3 (continued)

Not-for-Profit "C"
Statement of Cash Flows
Year Ended December 31, 20X4
(in thousands)

Investment in term endowment	50
Investment in plant	1,300
	1,650
Other financing activities:	
Interest and dividends restricted for reinvestment	55
Payments on notes payable	(1,040)
Payments on long-term debt	(1,100)
	(2,085)
Net cash used by financing activities	(435)
Net decrease in cash and cash equivalents	(10,480)
Cash and cash equivalents at beginning of year	10,530
Cash and cash equivalents at end of year	$ 50
Supplemental data:	
Noncash investing and financing activities:	
Gifts of equipment	$ 240
Gift of paid-up life insurance, cash surrender value	50
Interest paid	521

Reporting expenses by function and nature in one location

All NFPs are required to present expenses by function and nature in one location after implementing ASU No. 2016-14. This information can be presented in the notes, in the statement of activities, or as a separate statement. Prior to ASU No. 2016-14, voluntary health and welfare entities were required to present a statement of functional expenses. They may now choose from one of the three options to report this information.

Exhibit 1-4 is an example of a separate statement used to present expenses by function and nature in one location titled a statement of functional expenses. This matrix format makes it easy to determine the extent to which resources are used for such things as salaries, travel, and supplies within a program area.

Exhibit 1-4

Not-for-Profit "D"
Statement of Functional Expenses
Year Ended December 31, 20X8
(in thousands)

| | Program | Supporting Services | | Total |
		Management and General	Fund-Raising	
Awards and grants	$50,632	$ —	$ —	$ 50,632
Salaries	2,720	9,471	12,076	24,267
Employee benefits	365	1,717	8,466	10,548
Payroll taxes	145	2,132	1,680	3,957
Professional fees	142	1,096	1,338	2,576
Supplies	72	628	1,618	2,318
Telephone	191	562	1,206	1,959
Postage and shipping	44	416	2,929	3,389
Occupancy	287	1,695	2,591	4,573
Information processing	656	562	1,549	2,767
Printing and publications	135	612	4,885	5,632
Meetings and conferences	719	1,085	2,167	3,971
Other travel	191	788	1,192	2,171
Other expenses	159	919	502	1,580
Depreciation	634	913	1,534	3,081
Total expenses	$ 57,092	$ 22,596	$ 43,733	$123,421

Relationships within the financial statements

Within the basic financial statements there are many relationships that exist. For example, the cash and cash equivalents number from the statement of financial position will also appear in the statement of cash flows.

Comparative financial information

NFP entities often use columns in their financial statements. Such an approach makes it difficult to include comparative financial information for each column, unless a complete set of statements is included for the prior year.

Sometimes, an entity will include only a total column from the prior year to provide comparative information. If the information provided does not constitute a comparative presentation in conformity with generally accepted accounting principles (GAAP), such information should be reported with an appropriate title such as "with summarized financial information for the year ended June 30, 20X1." A note disclosure would also be required.

Reporting formats

NFP entities have a lot of flexibility in presenting information in their financial statements. One aspect of this flexibility is to report disaggregated information by using columns in the financial statements. Entities may use several columns to present information as long as the certain totals for the entity are reported. For example, the statement of financial position must report total assets, total liabilities, and total net assets, as well as totals for the two classes of net assets.

Entities may report columns in the financial statements to convey a variety of information. Some of the approaches used are as follows:

- *Net asset class*. Advantages of reporting the statement of activities in this format is that total contributions for the entity are shown, and the reclassifications between classes of net assets are easy to see. Exhibit 1-2 (shown earlier) is an example of a statement of activities with columns for each class of net assets. Some NFPs also use this format for the statement of financial position.
- *Operating based formats*. Some entities find it useful to break out operating activities from other activities. For example, exhibit 1-5 helps users understand the degree to which operations are dependent upon contributions. Other operating type formats could include the following:
  - *Operating and plant*. Some entities find it useful to show activities and balances related to land, building, and equipment separate from their operating activities.
  - *Operating and investments*. Some entities have substantial amounts in endowment and similar types of investments and find it helpful to report this information separately.
- *Fund information*. Exhibit 1-6 is an example of a balance sheet with columns for each fund. For some entities, fund information remains important for external financial reporting.

Entities also have the flexibility of different columns among the financial statements. For example, an entity may only have one column in the statement of financial position and use three columns in the statement of activities to report information by net asset class.

The examples we have discussed are just some of the ways an entity may display information in the financial statements. Again, entities have a significant amount of flexibility in financial statement formats. However, in all cases, entities must report the basic information that focuses on the entity as a whole.

Exhibit 1-5

	Net assets without donor restrictions	Net assets with donor restrictions	Total
Not-for-Profit "E" Statement of Activities Year Ended December 31, 20X8 (in thousands)			
Operating revenues			
Symphony activities			
Box office and tour	$70,500		$70,500
Media and other revenues	10,502		10,502
Theatrical presentations	5,025		5,025
Interest and dividends	3,030		3,030
Other income	1,208		1,208
Total operating revenues	90,265		90,265
Operating expenses			
Program expenses			
Symphony activities			
Performances	110,150		110,150
New productions	5,203		5,203
Other expenses	1,414		1,414
Theatrical presentations	8,222		8,222
	124,989		124,989
Supporting services			
Symphony Hall	7,556		7,556
General management	9,652		9,652
	17,208		17,208
Total operating expenses	142,197		142,197
Loss from operations	(51,932)		(51,932)

Exhibit 1-5 (continued)

Not-for-Profit "E"
Statement of Activities
Year Ended December 31, 20X8
(in thousands)

	Net assets without donor restrictions	Net assets with donor restrictions	Total
Contributions	52,017	$10,435	62,452
Net assets released from restrictions			
Satisfaction of program restrictions	1,515	(1,515)	
Expiration of time restrictions	5,968	(5,968)	
	59,500	2,952	62,452
Fund-raising expenses	(15,005)		(15,005)
	44,495	2,952	47,447
Change in net assets	(7,437)	2,952	(4,485)
Net assets			
Beginning of year	52,817	65,092	117,909
End of year	45,380	68,044	113,424

Exhibit 1-6

Not-for-Profit "F"
Balance Sheet
December 31, 20X8
(in thousands)

	A Fund	B Fund	Total
Assets:			
Cash	$12,432	695	$ 13,127
Contributions receivable	8,712	14,246	22,958
Investments	8,315		8,315
Inventories	3,670		3,670
Prepaid expenses	5,357		5,357
Land, buildings, and equipment	5,450		5,450
Total assets	$43,936	14,941	$58,877
Liabilities and net assets:			
Accounts payable	$ 9,752		$ 9,752
Accrued expenses	505		505
Deferred member dues	15,045		15,045
Notes payable	8,399		8,399
Total liabilities	33,701		33,701
Net assets:			
Without donor restrictions	8,233	7,419	15,652
With donor restrictions	2,002	7,522	2,002
Total net assets	10,235	14,941	25,176
Total liabilities and net assets	$43,936	$14,941	$58,877

Notes to the financial statements

NFP entities are subject to many of the same notes to the financial statements as any business enterprise. However, FASB ASC's incremental industry-specific guidance for not-for-profits also contains requirements specifically for NFPs. For example:

- FASB ASC 958-205-50 requires that if an NFP discloses in its financial statements a ratio of fund-raising expenses to amounts raised, it also shall disclose how it computes that ratio.
- FASB ASC 958-360-50 requires that an NFP that does not recognize and capitalize its collections or that capitalizes collections prospectively shall describe its collections, including their relative significance, and its stewardship policies for collections. If collection items not capitalized are de-accessed during the period, it also shall describe the items given away, damaged, destroyed, lost, or otherwise de-accessed during the period or disclose their fair value.
- FASB ASC 958-605-50 requires that an entity that receives contributed services shall describe the programs or activities for which those services were used, including the nature and extent of contributed services received for the period and the amount recognized as revenues for the period. Entities are encouraged to disclose the fair value of contributed services received but not recognized as revenues if that is practicable. The nature and extent of contributed services received can be described by nonmonetary information, such as the number and trends of donated hours received or service outputs provided by volunteer efforts, or other monetary information, such as the dollar amount of contributions raised by volunteers. Disclosure of contributed services is required regardless of whether the services received are recognized as revenue in the financial statements.
- The pending content in FASB ASC 958-210-50-1A requires an NFP to disclose both qualitative and quantitative information about how it manages it liquid resources.

In FASB ASC topics, section 50 (XXX-YY-50) contains specific disclosure requirements for a subtopic. It does not include general disclosure requirements that may reside in the *Notes to Financial Statements* topic of FASB ASC and other general presentation topics. This section may include references to general disclosure requirements that encompass the items addressed by the subtopic.

Investments and investment income

Investments commonly held by NFPs

NFP entities acquire various kinds of investments by contribution or purchase. These investments can be divided into the following four broad categories:

1	Investments in equity securities with readily determinable fair values (other than consolidated subsidiaries and equity securities reported under the equity method) and all investments in debt securities, which are investments that are subject to the requirements of FASB ASC 958-320
2	Investments that are accounted for under the equity method
3	Investments in derivative instruments that are subject to the requirements of FASB ASC 815 (If an investment would otherwise be in the scope of FASB ASC 958-320 and it has within it an embedded derivative that is subject to FASB ASC 815, the host contract [as described in FASB ASC 815-15-05-1] remains within the scope of FASB ASC 958-320.)
4	Other investments, which are those included in the scope of FASB ASC 958-325 (For example, certain investments in real estate, mortgage notes that are not debt securities, venture capital funds, certain partnership interests, oil and gas interests, and certain equity securities that do not have a readily determinable fair value. Other investments do not include investments described in the preceding three items or investments in consolidated subsidiaries.)

Initial recognition

Pursuant to FASB ASC 958-320-30-1, debt and equity securities are initially measured at their acquisition cost (excluding brokerage and other transaction fees) if they are purchased, and at fair value if they are received as a contribution or through an agency transaction. Pursuant to FASB ASC 958-325-30-1, other investments are initially measured at their acquisition cost (including brokerage and other transaction fees) if they are purchased, and at fair value if they are received as a contribution or through an agency transaction. Pursuant to FASB ASC 815-10-30, all derivative instruments are measured initially at fair value. Investments that are accounted for under the equity method are generally measured initially at cost pursuant to FASB ASC 323-10-30, although FASB ASC 970-323-30 provides more specific guidance for real estate ventures, and FASB ASC 323-10-30-2 requires initial measurement at fair value for the following:

1. A retained investment in the common stock of an investee (including a joint venture) in a deconsolidation transaction in accordance with paragraphs 810-10-40-3A through 40-5

2. An investment in the common stock of an investee (including a joint venture) recognized upon the derecognition of a distinct nonfinancial asset or distinct in substance nonfinancial asset in accordance with FASB ASC 610-20

Knowledge check

5. Which is accurate of the initial measurement of investments?

    a. Debt and equity securities are initially measured at their acquisition cost if they are purchased.
    b. Investments that are contributed are measured at donor's cost.
    c. Derivative instruments are not measured at fair value.
    d. All investments are initially recorded at cost.

Investment income

Investment revenue is reported on the statement of activities. It includes dividends, interest, rents, royalties, and similar payments on assets held as investments.

Per FASB ASC 958-320-45-1, dividend, interest, and other investment income should be reported in the period earned as increases or decreases in net assets without donor restrictions unless the use of the assets received is limited by donor-imposed restrictions. Donor-restricted investment income should be reported as an increase in net assets with donor restrictions, depending on the type of restriction.

All NFPs report investment return net of external and direct internal investment expenses. Requiring an NFP to report its investment return net of external and direct internal investment expenses provides a more comparable measure of investment returns across all NFPs, regardless of whether their investment activities (1) are managed by internal staff, outside investment managers, volunteers, or a combination, or (2) employ the use of mutual funds, hedge funds, or other vehicles for which management fees are embedded in the investment return of the vehicle. After the implementation of ASU No. 2016-14, there is no longer a requirement to disclose netted expenses. Removing this disclosure will help eliminate the difficulties and related costs in identifying embedded fees, and the resultant inconsistencies in the reported amounts of investment expenses.

Knowledge check

6. Which is accurate of investment income?

    a. Investment income excludes dividends.
    b. If there are no donor-imposed restrictions on the use of the income, it should be reported as an increase in net assets with donor restrictions.
    c. Investment income includes interest.
    d. Investment income excludes gains.

Unrealized and realized gains and losses

Unrealized gains and losses arise from changes in the fair value of investments, exclusive of dividend and interest income recognized but not yet received and exclusive of any write-down of the carrying amount of investments for impairment. Unrealized gains and losses are recognized in some circumstances (for example, when the investments are carried at fair value), but not in others (for example, when the investments are carried at cost). However, there are circumstances (for example, impairment) in which unrealized losses on investments carried at cost should be recognized.

Realized gains and losses arise from selling or otherwise disposing of investments. If realized gains and losses arise from selling or otherwise disposing of investments for which unrealized gains and losses have been recognized in the statement of activities of prior reporting periods, the amounts reported in the statement of activities as gains or losses upon the sale or other disposition of the investments should exclude the amount that has previously been recognized in the statement of activities. However, the components of that gain or loss may be reported as the realized amount (the difference between amortized cost and the sales proceeds) and the unrealized amount recognized in prior reporting periods. Exhibit 1-7 illustrates this reporting.

Exhibit 1-7: Reporting gains and losses

Facts

1. In 20X1, an NFP entity with a December 31 year-end purchases an equity security with a readily determinable fair value for $5,000.
2. At December 31, 20X1, the fair value of the security is $7,000.
3. During 20X2, the security is sold for $11,000.

Reporting gains and losses

20X1	Recognize a $2,000 unrealized gain and adjust the carrying value to $7,000. (The reported unrealized gain equals $7,000 fair value less $5,000 carrying value.)
20X2	Recognize a $4,000 realized gain and adjust the carrying value to zero. (The realized gain may be reported as the net of $11,000 selling price less the $7,000 carrying value at the time the security was sold.)

To the extent that investment gains and losses are recognized, they should be reported in the statement of activities as increases or decreases in net assets without donor restrictions, unless their use is by explicit donor stipulations or by law. In such cases, they should be reported in the statement of activities as increases or decreases in net assets with donor restrictions.

Knowledge check

7. Which is accurate of realized gains and losses?

    a. Realized gains and losses arise from selling or otherwise disposing of investments.
    b. If realized gains and losses arise from selling or otherwise disposing of investments for which unrealized gains and losses have been recognized in the statement of activities of prior reporting periods, the amounts reported in the statement of activities as gains or losses upon the sale or other disposition of the investments should include the amount that has previously been recognized in the statement of activities.
    c. Realized gains and losses should not be reported in the statement of activities.
    d. Unrealized gains and losses should be reported in the statement of financial position as a separate line item.

Valuation subsequent to acquisition

As illustrated in the following table, the valuation of investments subsequent to acquisition depends in part on the type of investment.

Valuation subsequent to acquisition	
Equity securities with readily determinable fair value (other than consolidated subsidiaries and equity securities reported under the equity method) and all debt securities	**Investments that are accounted for under the equity method or a fair value election**
FASB ASC 958-320-35-1 requires that investments in equity securities with readily determinable fair value and all investments in debt securities be measured at fair value in the statement of financial position.	Various investments can fall into this category and the guidance regarding valuation subsequent to acquisition is difficult to summarize.
Derivative instruments	**Other investments**
FASB ASC 815-10-25-1 and FASB ASC 815-10-35-1 require that investments in derivative instruments be reported as either assets or liabilities depending on the rights or obligations under the contracts and should be subsequently re-measured at fair value. Similarly, an embedded derivative shall be separated from the host contract and accounted for as a derivative instrument pursuant to FASB ASC 815-10 if and only if all of the criteria in FASB ASC 815-15-25-1 are met.	Guidance concerning the carrying amounts of other investments subsequent to acquisition differs depending upon the type of NFP.

Investment pools

An NFP may pool part or all of its investments (including investments arising from contributions with different kinds of restrictions) for portfolio management purposes. The number and the nature of the pools may vary from entity to entity.

When a pool is established, ownership interests are initially assigned (typically through unitization) to the various pool categories (sometimes referred to as *participants*) based on the market value of the cash and securities placed in the pool by each participant. Current market value is used to determine the number of units allocated to additional assets placed in the pool and to value withdrawals from the pool. Investment income and realized gains and losses (and any recognized unrealized gains and losses) are allocated equitably based on the number of units assigned to each participant.

Net assets of an endowment fund

As discussed in FASB ASC 958-205-45, an NFP shall report the net assets of an endowment fund in a statement of financial position within the two classes of net assets based on the existence or absence of donor-imposed restrictions. Some examples of endowment funds are the following:

Net assets with donor restrictions (perpetual)	Net assets with donor restrictions (time)	Net assets without donor restrictions
For example, the portion of a perpetual endowment that must be maintained in perpetuity — not used up, expended, or otherwise exhausted — is classified as net assets with donor restrictions that are perpetual.	For example, the portion of a term endowment that must be maintained for a specified term is classified as net assets with donor restrictions due to time restrictions.	For example, a board-designated endowment, which results from an internal designation on net assets without donor restrictions, is not donor-restricted and is classified as net assets without donor restrictions.

Donor-restricted endowment funds

Classification of donor-restricted endowment funds subject to UPMIFA

When classifying a donor-restricted endowment fund, consideration shall be given to both the donor's explicit stipulations and the applicable laws that extend donor restrictions. Investment return generally is considered free of donor restrictions unless its use is limited by a donor-imposed restriction or by law. In the United States, most donor-restricted endowment funds are subject to an enacted version of the Uniform Prudent Management of Institutional Funds Act of 2006 (UPMIFA) that extends a donor's restriction to use of the funds, including the investment return, until the funds are appropriated for expenditure by the governing board. Thus, if a donor or law imposes a restriction on the investment return, those returns shall be reported within net assets with donor restrictions until appropriated for expenditure. Conversely, for an endowment fund that is created by a governing board (board-designated endowment fund), assuming no other purpose-type restrictions exist on the use of those funds, that original fund and all investment returns are free of donor restrictions and shall be reported in net assets without donor restrictions.

In the absence of interpretation of the phrase *appropriated for expenditure* in subsection 4(a) of UPMIFA by legal or regulatory authorities, for purposes of the guidance related to presentation of financial statements, appropriation for expenditure is deemed to occur upon approval for expenditure, unless approval is for a future period, in which case appropriation is deemed to occur when that period is reached. Approval for expenditure may occur through different means within and across NFPs. Upon appropriation for expenditure, the time restriction expires to the extent of the amount appropriated and, in the absence of any purpose restrictions, results in a reclassification of that amount to net assets without donor restrictions. If the fund is also subject to a purpose restriction, the reclassification of the appropriated amount to net assets without donor restrictions shall not occur until that purpose restriction also has been met.

An underwater endowment is a donor-restricted endowment fund for which the fair value of the fund is less than either the original gift amount or the amount requires to be maintained by the donor or by law that extends donor restrictions. In the absence of donor stipulations or law to the contrary, losses on the investments of a donor-restricted endowment fund shall reduce net assets with donor restrictions.

In initially applying the guidance related to presentation of financial statements to a donor-restricted endowment fund in existence when an enacted version of the UPMIFA is first effective practitioners should consult FASB ASC 958-205-45.

Financial statement presentation

Gains and investment income that are limited to specific uses by donor-imposed restrictions may be reported as increases in net assets without donor restrictions if the restrictions are met in the same reporting period as the gains and income are recognized, provided that the entity has a similar policy for reporting contributions received, reports consistently from period to period, and discloses its accounting policy in the notes to the financial statements.

Realized and unrealized losses on investments may be netted against realized and unrealized gains on a statement of activities.

Some NFP entities, in managing their endowment funds, use a spending rate or total return policy. Those policies consider total investment return — investment income (interest, dividends, rents, and so forth) plus net realized and unrealized gains (or minus net losses). Typically, spending rate or total return policies emphasize the use of prudence and a rational and systematic formula to determine the portion of cumulative investment return that can be used to support operations of the current period and the protection of endowment gifts from a loss of purchasing power as a consideration in determining the formula to be used.

An NFP shall disclose information to enable users of financial statements to understand the net asset classification, net asset composition, changes in net asset composition, spending policies, and related investment policies. At a minimum, an NFP shall disclose all of the following information for each period for which it presents financial statements:

a. A description of the governing board's interpretation of the law or laws that underlie the NFP's net asset classification of donor-restricted endowment funds, including its interpretation of the ability to spend from underwater endowment funds.
b. A description of the NFP's policy or policies for the appropriation of endowment assets for expenditure (its endowment spending policy or policies), including its policy, and any actions taken during the period, concerning appropriation from underwater endowment funds.
c. A description of the NFP's endowment investment policies, including all of the following:
    i. Return objectives and risk parameters
    ii. How return objectives relate to the NFP's endowment spending policy or policies
    iii. The strategies employed for achieving return objectives
d. The composition of the NFP's endowment by net asset class at the end of the period, in total and by type of endowment fund, showing donor-restricted endowment funds separately from board-designated endowment funds.
e. A reconciliation of the beginning and ending balance of the NFP's endowment, in total and by net asset class, including, at a minimum, all of the following line items that apply:
    i. Investment return, net
    ii. Contributions
    iii. Amounts appropriated for expenditure that contain no purpose restrictions
    iv. Other changes.

Summary

The general purpose financial statements required by FASB ASC for an NFP entity are as follows: the statement of financial position, the statement of activities, the statement of cash flows, and accompanying notes to the financial statements. NFP entities must also present an analysis of expenses by function and nature in one location. This may be presented in the notes, in the statement of activities, or as a separate statement.

NFP entities have significant flexibility in presenting information in the financial statements. They can use separate columns to display information as long as certain totals for the entity are reported. There are also unique notes to the financial statements for NFP entities.

Many NFP entities hold endowment funds. The NFP reports the net assets of an endowment fund in a statement of financial position within the two classes of net assets based on the existence or absence of donor-imposed restrictions.

Practice questions

1. Which is a class of net assets for NFP entities?

    a. Net assets unrestricted.
    b. Net assets designated.
    c. Net assets with donor restrictions.
    d. Net assets permanently restricted.

2. The governing board decides to set up a board-designated endowment to be used for a specific operating purpose. In the statement of net assets, the board-designated endowment should be reported as

    a. Unrestricted net assets.
    b. Endowment net assets.
    c. Net assets without donor restrictions.
    d. Net assets with donor restrictions.

3. The statement of activities is required to report which item?

    a. Change in net assets without donor restrictions.
    b. Change in net assets.
    c. Change in net assets with donor restrictions.
    d. All of the above.

4. The statement of cash flows would report a cash contribution restricted in use for the future construction of a new building as cash inflow from

    a. Operating activities.
    b. Investing activities.
    c. Financing activities.
    d. A noncash disclosure.

5. If an entity uses the indirect method in their statement of cash flows to explain cash flows from operating activities, it must begin with which amount?

    a. Change in net assets.
    b. Operating income.
    c. Change in net assets without donor restrictions.
    d. Net income.

6. Which not-for-profit entity must report an analysis of expenses by function and nature in one location?

    a. College.
    b. Labor union.
    c. Voluntary health and welfare entity.
    d. All NFPs.

---

7. Which item is required to be reported in the statement of financial position?

    a. Total net assets.
    b. Total assets.
    c. Net assets with donor restrictions.
    d. All of the above.

Case study: Seaside Performing Arts, Inc.

Case Study: Background information

Seaside Performing Arts, Inc. (SPA) is a private NFP located in the eastern shore of Virginia. The entity owns a local theater that is an historic landmark. It can hold 400 people. The entity supports the area's symphony and several theatrical performances a year. Ticket prices for both the symphony and theatrical performances do not cover the costs of these productions. SPA depends on private contributions to cover approximately one-third of the costs of operations.

Recently, SPA hired Bob Singleton as their accountant. Bob is a business graduate of the local community college and has five years of accounting experience with the town of Accomac. He is familiar with fund accounting used by local governments, but is new to the reporting requirements of NFPs. With the help of his accounting textbook from college, Bob has prepared the statement of operations for the year just ended.

His textbook is not updated for the reporting requirements of ASU No. 2016-14. He has elected to report the functional classification of expenses on the face of the statement.

Case study: Seaside Performing Arts, Inc. (continued)

The following is the statement of operations prepared by Bob.

Seaside Performing Arts, Inc.
Statement of Operations
Year ended December 31, 201X
(in thousands)

	Unrestricted	Temporarily restricted	Permanently restricted
Operating revenues			
Symphony activities			
Box office and tour	$70,000		
Media and other revenues	10,500		
Theatrical presentations	5,000		
Interest and dividends	3,000		
Other income	1,200		
Total operating revenues	89,700		
Operating expenditures			
Program expenditures			
Symphony activities			
Performances	110,000	2,400	
New productions	5,200	3,500	
Other expenditures	1,400		
Theatrical presentations	8,000	1,500	
	124,600	7,400	
Supporting services			
Symphony Hall	7,500		
General management	9,600		
	17,100	—	
Total operating expenditures	141,700	7,400	
Loss from operations	(52,000)	(7,400)	

Case study: Seaside Performing Arts, Inc. (continued)

Seaside Performing Arts, Inc.
Statement of Operations
Year ended December 31, 201X
(in thousands)

	Unrestricted	Temporarily Restricted	Permanently Restricted
Contributions	$82,400		
Less:			
Transfers of restricted gifts	(10,400)	9,000	1,400
Depreciation	(12,500)		
Fund-raising expenditures	(15,000)		
Other support and expenditures	44,500	9,000	1,400
Change in net assets	(7,500)	1,600	1,400
Net assets			
Beginning of year	52,800	15,000	50,000
End of year	$ 45,300	$ 16,600	$ 51,400

Case study exercise

Review the statement prepared by Bob. Describe any deficiencies you observe in the statement.

List any changes to this statement from the implementation of FASB ASU No. 2016-14.

Chapter 2

Exchange Transactions, Contributions, and Gains and Losses

Learning objectives

- Identify key concepts regarding exchange (reciprocal) transactions.

- Identify some of the critical characteristics of contributions and the conditions and restrictions that may be placed upon them.

- Identify how to recognize and report promises to give and contributed services.

Introduction

All engines need some type of fuel to function. Not-for-profits (NFPs) also need fuel (that is, resources) to function and achieve their mission. Exchange transactions and contributions are key sources of fuel that power NFPs to make a vital difference in our society and the world. In this chapter, we will discuss exchange transactions and contributions and how they are accounted for and reported. We will also address the concept of agency transactions.

In June 2018, FASB issued Accounting Standards Update (ASU) No. 2018-08, *Clarifying the Scope and the Accounting Guidance for Contributions Received and Contributions Made.* This standard is intended to clarify and improve current guidance about whether a transfer of assets is an exchange transaction or a contribution. If the donors or grantors receive commensurate value in return for the resources provided, the asset transfer is an exchange (reciprocal) transaction.

For contributions (nonreciprocal transactions), the standard requires that an entity determine whether a contribution is conditional based on whether an agreement includes a barrier that must be overcome and either a right of return of assets transferred or a right of release of a promisor's obligation to transfer assets. Conditional contributions are recognized as liabilities or not recognized at all until the barriers are overcome, at which point the transaction is recognized as unconditional and classified as either net assets with restrictions or net assets without restrictions. Unconditional contributions are recognized as revenue when received. This chapter reflects the requirements of ASU No. 2018-08.

Resources for the mission

NFPs receive inflows of resources from a variety of sources as shown in exhibit 2-1.

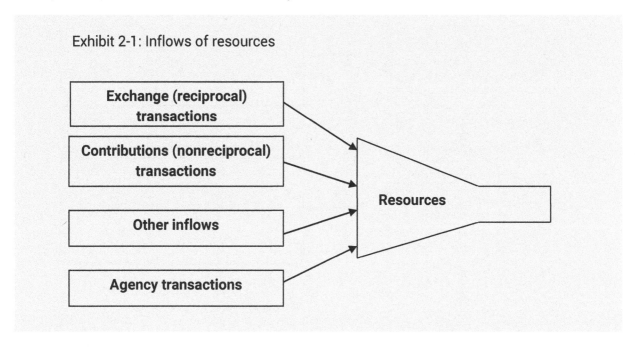

Exhibit 2-1: Inflows of resources

How these resources are classified will result in differences in how they are recognized and reported. As shown in exhibit 2-1, the inflow of resources can come from the following:

- *Exchange (reciprocal) transactions.* Inflows from exchange transactions arise when both parties receive goods and services of commensurate value.
- *Contributions (nonreciprocal) transactions.* Inflows from an unconditional transfer of assets, as well as unconditional promises to give, or reduction, settlement, or cancellation of debt in a voluntary nonreciprocal transfer by an entity other than an owner.
- *Other inflows.* NFPs receive resources from other activities such as investment activities.
- *Agency transactions.* Inflows from transfers in which the entity is acting as an agent, trustee, or other intermediary for the donor.

Exhibit 2-2 is a flowchart that provides guidance for determining whether a transfer of assets includes a contribution.

Exhibit 2-2: Determining whether a transfer to an NFP includes a contribution[1]

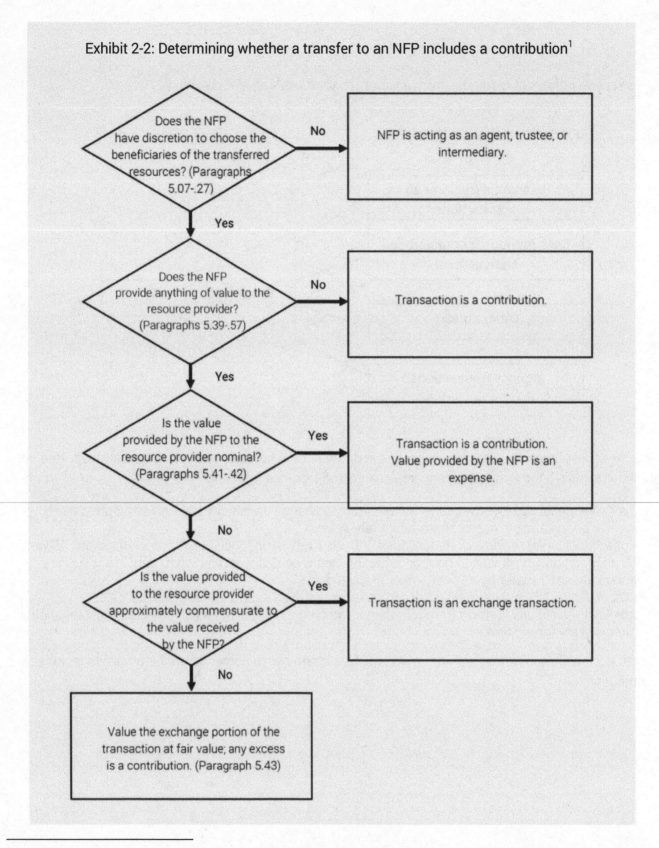

Knowledge check

1. Which is accurate of the resources received by NFP entities?

    a. NFPs receive resources from activities such as investment activities.
    b. NFP entities receive inflows of resources from a limited number of sources.
    c. Inflows from transfers in which the entity is acting as an agent, trustee, or other intermediary for the donor are not referred to as agency transactions.
    d. NFPs do not engage in exchange (reciprocal) transactions.

Exchange (reciprocal) transactions

Exchange (reciprocal) transactions are transfers in which each party receives and sacrifices something of commensurate value. For example, fees charged for providing goods and services to members, clients, students, and customers that receive commensurate benefits are revenues from exchange transactions. This is similar to how a business enterprise would define revenue.

The core principle of the revised revenue recognition standard is that an entity should recognize revenue to depict the transfer of goods or services to customers in an amount that reflects the consideration to which the entity expects to be entitled in exchange for those good or services.

To apply the revenue recognition standard, ASU No. 2014-09, *Revenue from Contracts with Customers (Topic 606)*, an entity should follow these five steps:

1. Identify the contracts with a customer.
2. Identify the performance obligations in the contract.
3. Determine the transaction price.
4. Allocate the transaction price to the performance obligations in the contract.
5. Recognize revenue when (or as) the entity satisfies a performance obligation.

Under the new standard, revenue is recognized when an entity satisfies a performance obligation by transferring a promised good or service to a customer (which is when the customer obtains control of that good or service).

In some situations, judgment is required to determine whether an increase in net assets should be reported as a revenue or as a gain. Exchange (reciprocal) transaction revenues result from an entity providing goods and services that are part of the entity's ongoing major or central activities. Revenues are different than gains. Gains result from activities that are peripheral or incidental to the entity. Some activities that are reported as revenue by some entities would be reported as gains by others. A library that has a major, annual book sale would report this activity as revenue, whereas a church that sells a cookbook as part of a 25-year anniversary celebration would likely report this activity as a gain.

It may be difficult to determine if an activity is peripheral or incidental to an entity or if the activity is part of the organization's ongoing major or central operations. In making this determination, an entity should consider the frequency of the events and the significance of the event's gross revenue and expenses. Events are considered ongoing major and central if

- they are normally part of an organization's strategy and it normally carries on such activities, or
- the event's gross revenues or expenses are significant in relation to the organization's annual budget.

Knowledge check

2. Which is accurate of exchange transactions?

    a. Exchange transaction revenues result from an entity providing goods and services that are part of the organization's ongoing major or central activities.

    b. Fees charged for providing goods and services to members, clients, students, and customers that receive substantive benefits are not revenues from exchange transactions.

    c. Judgment is not required to determine whether an increase in net assets should be reported as revenue or as a gain.

    d. A transaction cannot be considered part exchange transaction and part contribution.

Five-step process

Step 1

Step 1 is to identify the contract with the customer. A contract is an agreement between two or more parties that creates enforceable rights and obligations. A contract can be written, oral, or implied by an entity's customary business practices. An entity should apply the requirements to each contract that meets the following criteria:

1. There is approval and commitment of the parties.
2. The rights of the parties have been identified.
3. The payment terms have been identified.
4. The contract has commercial substance.
5. It is probable that the entity will collect the consideration to which it will be entitled in exchange for the goods or services that will be transferred to the customer.

Step 2

Step 2 is to identify the performance obligations in the contract.

A performance obligation is a promise in a contract with a customer to transfer a good or service to the customer. If an entity promises in a contract to transfer more than one good or service to the customer, the entity should account for each promised good or service as a performance obligation only if it is (1) distinct or (2) a series of distinct goods or services that are substantially the same and have the same pattern of transfer.

A good or service is distinct if both of the following criteria are met:

1. *It is capable of being distinct.* The customer can benefit from the good or service either on its own or together with other resources that are readily available to the customer.
2. *It is distinct within the context of the contract.* The promise to transfer the good or service is separately identifiable from other promises in the contract.

A good or service that is not distinct should be combined with other promised goods or services until the entity identifies a bundle of goods or services that is distinct.

The following are examples of promised goods or services (performance obligations):

- Sale of goods produced by an entity
- Resale of goods purchased by an entity
- Constructing, manufacturing, or developing an asset on behalf of a customer
- Granting licenses

Step 3

Step 3 is to determine the transaction price. The transaction price is the amount of consideration to which an entity expects to be entitled in exchange for transferring promised goods or services to a customer, excluding amounts collected on behalf of third parties.

To determine the transaction price, an entity should consider the following:

Is the amount of consideration variable?

In the case of variable consideration, the entity will need to estimate the amount to include in the transaction price using either the expected value (that is, the probability-weighted amount) or the most likely amount, depending on which method management expects will better predict the amount of consideration to which the entity will be entitled. FASB specifies that the estimate of variable consideration should be included in the transaction price only to the extent it is probable that no significant reversal in the amount of cumulative revenue recognized will occur when the uncertainty associated with the variable consideration is subsequently resolved.

If the expected time to receive payment is more than one year from the transfer of the promised goods or services, is there a significant financing component?

An entity should adjust the promised amount of consideration for the effects of the time value of money if the timing of the payments agreed upon by the parties to the contract (either explicitly or implicitly) provides the customer or the entity with a significant benefit of financing for the transfer of goods or services to the customer. In assessing whether a financing component exists and is significant to a contract, an entity should consider various factors. As a practical expedient, an entity need not assess whether a contract has a significant financing component if the entity expects at contract inception that the period between payment by the customer and the transfer of the promised goods or services to the customer will be one year or less.

Has the customer promised noncash consideration?

Noncash consideration (or promise thereof) should be measured at fair value. If an entity cannot reasonably estimate the fair value of the noncash consideration, it should measure the consideration indirectly using the stand-alone selling price of the goods or services promised in exchange for the consideration.

Is there consideration payable to the customer?

If an entity pays, or expects to pay, consideration to a customer in the form of cash or items (for example, a coupon, credit, or voucher) that the customer can apply against amounts owed, the entity should account for the payment (or expectation of payment) as a reduction of the transaction price, as a payment for a distinct good or service, or both.

Step 4

Step 4 is to allocate the transaction price to each performance obligation in the contract in an amount that depicts the consideration to which the entity expects to be entitled in exchange for satisfying each performance obligation.

To do this, an entity must determine the stand-alone selling price at contract inception of the distinct goods or services underlying each performance obligation. The transaction price then would typically be allocated on a relative stand-alone selling price basis.

If a stand-alone selling price is not observable, an entity must estimate it.

Sometimes, the transaction price includes a discount or variable consideration that relates entirely to one of the performance obligations in a contract. The requirements specify when an entity should allocate the discount or variable consideration to one or more performance obligations rather than to all performance obligations in the contract.

An entity should allocate to the performance obligations in the contract any subsequent changes in the transaction price on the same basis as at contract inception. Amounts allocated to a satisfied performance obligation should be recognized as revenue, or as a reduction of revenue, in the period in which the transaction price changes.

Step 5

Step 5 is to recognize revenue when (or as) the performance obligations are satisfied. A performance obligation is satisfied by transferring a promised good or service to a customer, and a good or service is transferred when (or as) the customer obtains control of that good or service.

For each performance obligation, an entity should determine whether the entity satisfies the performance obligation over time by transferring control of a good or service over time, that is, by determining if one of the following criteria is met:

1. The customer simultaneously receives and consumes the benefits provided by the entity's performance as the entity performs.
2. The entity's performance creates or enhances an asset (for example, work in process) that the customer controls as the asset is created or enhanced.
3. The entity's performance does not create an asset with an alternative use to the entity, and the entity has an enforceable right to payment for performance completed to date.

If a performance obligation is not satisfied over time, an entity satisfies the performance obligation at a point in time. To determine the point in time at which a customer obtains control of a promised asset and an entity satisfies a performance obligation, the entity would consider indicators of the transfer of control, which include, but are not limited to, the following:

1. The entity has a present right to payment for the asset.
2. The customer has legal title to the asset.
3. The entity has transferred physical possession of the asset.
4. The customer has the significant risks and rewards of ownership of the asset.
5. The customer has accepted the asset.

For each performance obligation that an entity satisfies over time, an entity should recognize revenue over time by consistently applying a method of measuring the progress toward complete satisfaction of that performance obligation. Appropriate methods of measuring progress include output methods and input methods. As circumstances change over time, an entity should update its measure of progress to depict the entity's performance completed to date.

Revenue recognition for exchange (reciprocal) transactions

The recognition, measurement, and display of revenues and related receivables arising from exchange (reciprocal) transactions are similar for both NFP and for-profit entities using accrual accounting. Revenue is recognized when a company satisfies a performance obligation by transferring a promised good or service to a customer (which is when the customer obtains control of that good or service). Revenues should be measured by the increase in cash, receivables, or other assets or by the decrease in liabilities resulting from the transaction. Revenues from exchange (reciprocal) transactions are reported as increases in net assets without donor restrictions in a statement of activities.

Revenues from exchange transactions are reported gross of any related expenses. If the entity regularly provides discounts (such as financial aid for students that is not reported as an expense, reduced fees for services, or free services) to certain recipients of its goods or services, revenues should be reported net of those discounts.

Receivables arising from exchange transactions should be reported at net realizable value if the amounts are due within one year. Long-term receivables should be reported in conformity with FASB ASC 310-10-35. Pursuant to FASB ASC 210-10-45-13, a valuation allowance for uncollectible receivables should be deducted from the receivables to which the allowance relates and should be disclosed.

Knowledge check

3. Which is accurate of revenue recognition for exchange (reciprocal) transactions?

    a. Revenues from exchange transactions should be recognized based on accrual accounting principles.
    b. The recognition, measurement, and display of revenues and related receivables arising from exchange transactions are not similar for NFP and for-profit entities.
    c. Revenues from exchange transactions should be reported as increases in net assets with donor restrictions in a statement of activities.
    d. Revenue should not be reported net of regularly provided discounts.

Distinguishing exchange transactions from contributions

As we will soon discuss, contributions are an unconditional transfer of cash or other assets, as well as unconditional promises to give, to an entity or a reduction, settlement, or cancellation of its liabilities in a voluntary nonreciprocal transfer by another entity acting other than as an owner. Sometimes an entity will give such things as calendars or mailing labels to potential donors. Also, some entities give things like coffee mugs or T-shirts to actual donors. Because something of value is given, does this make it an exchange transaction? Generally no, if the items given are of nominal value. In such cases, the full amount received would be considered a contribution and the cost of the items given would be a fund-raising expense.

Is it possible for a transaction to be considered part exchange and part contribution? Yes. For example, if the item given to a donor has more than nominal value, but is less than the value of the donation received, the transaction would be considered part exchange and part contribution.

In determining whether a transfer of assets is an exchange transaction in which a resource provider (for example, a government agency, a foundation, a corporation, or other entity) receives commensurate value in return for the resources transferred or a contribution, the type of resource provider shall not factor into the determination and an entity shall evaluate the terms of an agreement and consider the following:

a. The resource provider (including a foundation, a government agency, a corporation, or other entity) is not synonymous with the general public. A benefit received by the public as a result of the assets transferred is not equivalent to commensurate value received by the resource provider. Therefore, if the resource provider receives indirect value in exchange for the assets transferred or if the value received by the resource provider is incidental to the potential public benefit from using the assets transferred, the transaction shall not be considered commensurate value received in return.
b. Execution of the resource provider's mission or the positive sentiment from acting as a donor shall not constitute commensurate value received by the resource provider for purposes of determining whether the transfer of assets is a contribution or an exchange.
c. If the expressed intent asserted by both the recipient and the resource provider is to exchange resources for goods or services that are of commensurate value, the transaction shall be indicative of an exchange transaction. The transaction shall be indicative of a contribution if the recipient solicits

assets from the resource provider without the intent of exchanging goods or services of commensurate value.

d. If the resource provider has full discretion in determining the amount of the transferred assets, the transaction shall be indicative of a contribution. If both the recipient and the resource provider agree on the amount of assets transferred in exchange for goods and services that are of commensurate value, the transaction shall be indicative of an exchange transaction.

e. If the penalties assessed on the recipient for failure to comply with the terms of the agreement are limited to the delivery of assets or services already provided and the return of the unspent amount, the transaction is generally indicative of a contribution. The existence of contractual provisions for economic forfeiture beyond the amount of assets transferred by the resource provider to penalize the recipient for nonperformance generally indicates that the transaction is an exchange of commensurate value.

A single transaction may be part exchange and part contribution. For example, an individual may enter into an agreement to transfer land to an NFP at a price substantially lower than fair value. Following the steps described earlier, the NFP would assign a price to the performance obligation for the transfer of the land. The difference between the price assigned to the land and the amount paid would be a contribution.

Some entities receive grants, awards, or sponsorships from other entities. Many of these are contributions, but some of these items may be exchange transactions. If the value received by the resource provider is nominal or incidental to the potential public benefit from the resource provided, the transaction would be considered a contribution. ASU No. 2018-08 explicitly states that societal benefit is not commensurate value, even if it furthers the resource provider's charitable mission

However, in some cases, grants, awards, or sponsorships are considered an exchange transaction. For example, a company may engage an NFP university to conduct research on the effects of a new drug. The company specifies the requirements for the research and also retains the rights to the results from the research.

Membership dues

Some entities receive dues from their members. These dues may be considered exchange, part exchange and part contribution, or all contribution. Classifying dues depends on tangible or intangible benefits received. For example, if an entity has a membership fee of $100 and the only tangible benefit a member receives is an annual publication with a fair value of $25, the entity would classify $75 of the dues as a contribution and $25 as an exchange transaction. If dues are classified as exchange transactions, they should be recognized as revenue as the earnings process is completed.

Revenue derived from membership dues in exchange transactions should be recognized over the period to which the dues relate. Nonrefundable initiation and life membership fees received in exchange transactions should be recognized as revenues in the period in which the fees become receivable if future fees are expected to cover the costs of future services to be provided to members. If nonrefundable initiation and life membership fees, rather than future fees, are expected to cover those costs, nonrefundable initiation and life member fees received in exchange transactions should be recognized as revenue over the average duration of membership, the life expectancy of members, or other appropriate time periods.

Naming opportunities

Many entities offer naming opportunities for resources providers. For example, a college may provide the opportunity to name a building or classroom for receiving a certain dollar amount. An entity needs to consider if the resources received are a contribution, exchange transactions or some combination of both.

If the public recognition and accompanying rights and privileges are nominal in value to the resource provided, the entity has received a contribution. However, the entity needs to consider specific facts and circumstances around the naming opportunity. Exhibit 2-3 contains a list of indicators that may be helpful in determining if a naming opportunity is a contribution, exchange transaction, or a combination of both. Some indicators may be more significant than others: however, no single indicator is determinative of the classification of a particular transaction.

Exhibit 2-3: Naming opportunities indicators useful in distinguishing contributions from exchange transactions

Indicator	Contribution	Exchange transaction
Value of public recognition	Resource provider receives nominal value related to the public recognition and there are no direct benefits provided to the resource provider.	Resource provider receives significant value related to the public recognition or there are direct benefits provided to the resource provider.
Length of time that the naming benefit is provided	Naming benefit is provided for a relatively short time, or the NFP has the right to change the name at its discretion.	Naming benefit is provided for relatively long time, and the name cannot be changed solely at the NFP's discretion.
Control over name and logo use	Party receiving the naming opportunity cannot change the name.	Party receiving the naming opportunity can change the name, such as if a corporate donor changes its name and requires a corresponding name change at the NFP.
Other rights and privileges	The named party receives no other rights or privileges in connection with the naming opportunity transaction.	The named party receives other rights and privileges in connection with the naming opportunity transaction, such as an exclusive right to sell, exclusive recruitment opportunities, and so forth.

Knowledge check

4. Which is accurate of distinguishing exchange transactions from contributions?

    a. Some entities receive grants, awards, or sponsorships from other entities. Many of these are contributions, but some of these items may be exchange transactions.
    b. If dues are classified as exchange transactions, they should not be recognized as revenue as the earnings process is completed.
    c. Some entities receive dues from their members. These dues can never be considered an exchange transaction.
    d. If items of nominal value are given, the transaction is reported as an exchange transaction.

Contributions

Individuals, foundations, businesses, and other entities make all kinds of donations to NFP entities. Donations can take the form of things such as cash or other assets, including securities, land, buildings, use of facilities or utilities, materials and supplies, intangible assets, services, and unconditional promises to give those items in the future. Contributions represent unconditional transfers of cash or other assets, as well as unconditional promises to give, to an entity or a reduction, settlement or cancellation of its liabilities in a voluntary nonreciprocal transfer by another entity acting other than as an owner. In a contribution transaction, the resource provider often receives value indirectly by providing a societal benefit, although the benefit is not considered to be of commensurate value.

Unconditional contributions received are recognized as revenue in the period received. Some contributions can come with conditions, restrictions, or both. This following section will cover when and how contributions are measured.

Conditional contributions

As stated previously, donations can contain conditions, restrictions, or both. ASU No. 2018-08 provides guidance on reporting conditional and restricted contributions. For contribution to be considered conditional, it must have both of the following:

1. One or more barriers that must be overcome before the NFP is entitled to the assets transferred or promised
2. A right of return to the contributor for assets transferred (or for a reduction, settlement, or cancellation of liabilities) or a right of release of the promisor from its obligation to transfer assets (or to reduce, settle, or cancel liabilities)

An NFP needs to consider facts and circumstances to determine if a barrier exists. To determine if an agreement contains a barrier, ASU No. 2018-08 provides the following indicators (some indicators may be more significant than others):

- The agreement requires the NFP to achieve a measurable outcome (for example, provide a specific number of units of output or meet a matching requirement).
- The NFP has little discretion over the conduct of the activity (for example, following requirements for incurring qualifying expenses or requiring the hiring of specific individuals).
- The agreement contains stipulations related to the purpose of the agreement (for example, providing a research report on the effects of certain allergies). This excludes trivial or administrative requirements.

A conditional contribution is different from a donor-imposed restriction that limits the use of a contribution to some specific purpose that is narrower than the broad nature and purpose of the organization.

An example of a conditional contribution is when a donor pledges $100,000 if the entity can raise an additional $100,000 in the next 12 months. It contains both a barrier and a right to be released from the promise to provide resources. An example of a restricted contribution is when a donor stipulates that a $10,000 gift must be used for a specific program of an organization.

> Donor-imposed conditions should be substantially met by the entity before the receipt of assets (including contributions receivable) is recognized as a contribution. A transfer of assets that is a conditional contribution is accounted for as a refundable advance until the conditions have been substantially met. Conditional promises to give are only recognized when the conditions are substantially met or explicitly waived by the donor.

Knowledge check

5. Which is accurate of conditional contributions?

   a. A conditional promise to give should be recognized only when the conditions are substantially met.
   b. A donor pledging $100,000 if the entity can raise an additional $100,000 in the next 12 months is an example of an unconditional contribution.
   c. Donor-imposed conditions should not be substantially met by the entity before the receipt of assets (including contributions receivable) is recognized as a contribution.
   d. Conditional promises to give cannot contain restrictions.

Restricted contributions

Contributions made to entities may or may not have donor-imposed restrictions. Donor-imposed restrictions (donors include other types of contribution such as certain grants) specify the use of a contributed asset that is more specific than the broad limits resulting from the nature of the NFP, the environment in which it operates, and the purposes specified in its articles of incorporation or bylaws or comparable documents for an unincorporated association. Donor-imposed restrictions can either perpetually or temporarily limit the use of contributed assets. Generally, restrictions are stipulated explicitly by the donor in a written or oral communication accompanying the gift. In addition to explicit donor-imposed restrictions, there are certain contributions that may have implied restrictions.

In addition to explicit donor-imposed restrictions, there are certain contributions that may have implied restrictions as follows:

- Restrictions that result implicitly from the circumstances surrounding the receipt of the contributed asset (for example, a contribution received in response to an appeal to raise resources for a new building).
- Contributions of unconditional promises to give with payments due in future periods should be reported as restricted contributions unless the donor expressly stipulates, or circumstances

surrounding the receipt of the promise make clear, that the donor intended it to be used to support activities of the current period.

Some entities receive contributions of long-lived assets (for example, equipment and buildings) or cash and other assets restricted to the purchase of long-lived assets. Often, the donor will not expressly stipulate how or how long the long-lived asset must be used by the organization. Absent donor stipulations specifying how long such donated assets or assets constructed or acquired with cash restricted for such acquisition or construction must be used, restrictions on long-lived assets, if any, expire when the assets are placed in service as required by FASB ASC 958-205-45-12.

Contributions with donor-imposed restrictions (explicit or implied) will increase net assets with donor restrictions. Contributions with no donor-imposed restrictions increase net assets without donor restrictions.

Some donor restrictions are perpetual in nature and limits the use of assets that neither expire by passage of time nor can be fulfilled or otherwise removed by the organization's action. For example, a gift of securities to establish an endowment. Some donor restrictions limit the use of assets by donor-imposed stipulations that either expire by passage of time (time restriction) or can be fulfilled and removed by actions of the entity pursuant to those stipulations (purpose restriction). For example, a restriction on a contribution to acquire certain equipment expires when the equipment is acquired by the organization.

In some cases, donor-imposed restrictions are met in the same period that the contribution is received. An entity may adopt an accounting policy that would report such contributions as net assets without donor restrictions. For example, suppose a library receives a donation during the year restricted to the purchase of books and expends those resources to purchase books during the same year. The library may adopt a policy to report such contributions as increases in net assets without donor restrictions. Such a policy would have to be consistent from period to period and properly disclosed in the notes to the financial statements. The entity would also have to have a similar policy for investment gains and income that have donor-imposed restrictions.

Knowledge check

6. Which is accurate of restricted contributions?

    a. Donor-imposed restrictions can either be purpose, time or perpetual in nature.
    b. Donor-imposed restrictions are never met in the same period that the contribution is received.
    c. Restrictions are not generally stipulated explicitly by the donor in a written or oral communication accompanying the gift.
    d. Contributions cannot have implied restrictions.

Promises to give

Unconditional promises to give cash or other assets in the future are contributions and would be reported as receivables and contribution revenues in the period the unconditional promises are made. An unconditional promise to give can be either a written or an oral agreement.

There should be sufficient verifiable evidence that an unconditional promise to give has been made. Such evidence may include written agreements and pledge cards. For oral promises, evidence can include tape recordings, written minutes, and follow-up written confirmations.

In addition to unconditional promises to give, some entities may also receive intentions to give. Intentions to give are not unconditional promises to give and would not be recorded because individuals retain the ability to rescind their intention to give. For example, an individual may indicate that an entity has been included in their will as a beneficiary. Because the individual retains the ability to change the will, this is considered an intention to give and would not be recorded. NFP entities should *disclose* information about conditional promises in valid wills.

Unconditional promises to give that are due in future periods generally increase net assets with donor restrictions, rather than net assets without donor restrictions. If, however, the donor explicitly stipulates that the promise to give is to support current-period activities or if other circumstances surrounding the promise make it clear that the donor's intention is to support current-period activities, unconditional promises to give should be reported as increases in net assets without donor restrictions.

Contributed services

Many NFP entities depend on volunteers for a variety of functions. Some contributed services should be recognized in the financial statements as illustrated in the following:

> **Contributed services should be reported as contribution revenue and as assets or expenses only if**
>
> - the services create or enhance a nonfinancial asset (for example, a building), or
> - all three of the following apply:
>   - The services require specialized skills (some examples of specialized skills are accounting, financial, educational, construction, electrical, legal, and medical).
>   - The services are provided by individuals with those skills.
>   - The services would typically need to be purchased by the entity if they had not been contributed.

Just because an individual has a specialized skill does not mean that it meets the criteria to be reported. For example, a CPA may volunteer for an entity in a position that does not require his or her CPA skills or create or enhance a nonfinancial asset. Therefore, this contributed service would not be reported in the financial statements. However, for example, if the CPA contributes his or her services to a position that requires those skills and typically the entity would have to pay for those services, it would be reported in the financial statements.

FASB ASC 958-720 provides additional guidance for the situation when service is contributed from employees of a separately governed affiliated entity. Specifically, it requires an NFP entity to recognize all services received from personnel of an affiliate that directly benefit the organization. Those services should be measured at the cost recognized by the affiliate for the personnel providing those services, or, if elected, at the fair value of the service because the measurement at cost will significantly overstate or understate the value of the service received.

The standard applies to NFP entities that receive services from personnel of an affiliate that directly benefit the recipient NFP entity and for which the affiliate does not charge the recipient NFP entity. Charging the recipient NFP entity means requiring payment from the recipient NFP entity at least for the approximate amount of the direct personnel costs (for example, compensation and any payroll-related fringe benefits) incurred by the affiliate in providing a service to the recipient NFP entity or the approximate fair value of that service.

Other contributions

Some entities receive noncash assets, which are often referred to as *gifts in kind*. Gifts in kind that can be used internally or sold should be reported as revenues at fair value. If the gift has no value (such as certain used clothing) and cannot be used internally (or for program purposes) or sold, the item received should not be recorded.

Some entities receive items that will be used for fund-raising purposes (such as tickets to events or gift certificates) as part of a fund-raising event. For example, tickets to a play may be donated to an entity that will auction them off as part of an annual fund-raising event. Such items should be recorded as contribution revenue at fair value when received. When the item is sold, the difference between the amount received and the amount the item was initially recorded at should be recorded as an adjustment to the original contribution. For example, a gift certificate with a fair value of $50 donated to an entity for a charity auction would initially be recorded as a contribution revenue of $50. If the item is sold at the auction for $40, a reduction of $10 in contribution revenue would be recorded.

NFPs may receive unconditional contributions of the use of electric, telephone, and other utilities and of long-lived assets (such as a building or the use of facilities) in which the donor retains legal title to the long-lived asset. Entities receiving such contributions should recognize contribution revenue in the period in which the contribution is received and expenses in the period the utilities or long-lived assets are used. If the transaction is an unconditional promise to give for a specified number of periods, the promise should be reported as contributions receivable and as restricted support that increases net assets with donor restrictions.

Unconditional promises to give the use of long-lived assets (such as a building or other facilities) for a specified number of periods in which the donor retains legal title to the long-lived asset may be received in connection with leases or may be similar to leases but have no lease payments. For example, NFP entities may use facilities under lease agreements that call for lease payments at amounts below the fair rental value of the property. In such circumstances, the NFP entity should report a contribution for the difference between the fair rental value of the property and the stated amount of the lease payments. (However, amounts reported as contributions should not exceed the fair value of the long-lived asset at the time the entity receives the unconditional promise to give.) The contribution receivable may be described in the financial statements based on the item whose use is being contributed, such as a building, rather than as contributions receivable.

Collections

Many entities hold certain assets that are collections. Collections represent works of art, historical treasures, or similar assets that meet all of the following criteria:

- They are held for public exhibition, education, or research in furtherance of public service rather than financial gain.
- They are protected, kept unencumbered, cared for, and preserved.
- They are subject to an organizational policy that requires the proceeds of items that are sold to be used to acquire other items for collections.

An entity can either adopt a policy of capitalizing collections or not capitalizing collections. If collections are capitalized, donations of items to the collection would be reported as contribution revenue based on the fair value of the item. If collections are not capitalized, no asset or contribution revenue would be recorded for donations of assets to the collection.

Measurement of contributions

Contribution revenue should be measured at the fair value of the assets or services received or promised or the fair value of the liabilities satisfied. (Contributions arising from unconditional promises to give that are expected to be collected within one year of the financial statement date may be measured at their net realizable value.) FASB ASC 820 defines fair value and establishes a framework for measuring fair value.

Exhibit 2-4: More information on FASB ASC 820

Definition of fair value

FASB ASC 820 defines *fair value* as "the price that would be received to sell an asset or paid to transfer a liability in an orderly transaction between market participants at the measurement date." A fair value measurement assumes that the transaction to sell the asset or transfer the liability occurs in the principal market for the asset or liability or, in the absence of a principal market, the most advantageous market for the asset or liability. FASB ASC 820-10-20 defines the *principal market* as the market with the greatest volume and level of activity for the asset or liability and the *most advantageous market* as the market that maximizes the amount that would be received to sell the asset or minimizes the amount that would be paid to transfer the liability, after taking into account transaction costs and transportation costs.

Valuation techniques

FASB ASC 820 describes the valuation techniques that should be used to measure fair value. Valuation techniques consistent with the market approach, income approach, and/or cost approach should be used to measure fair value, as follows:

- The market approach uses prices and other relevant information generated by market transactions involving identical or comparable assets or liabilities. Valuation techniques consistent with the market approach include matrix pricing and often use market multiples derived from a set of comparables.
- The income approach uses valuation techniques to convert future amounts (for example, cash flows or earnings) to a single present amount (discounted). The measurement is based on the value indicated by current market expectations about those future amounts. Valuation techniques consistent with the income approach include present value techniques, option-pricing models, and the multi-period excess earnings method.
- The cost approach is based on the amount that currently would be required to replace the service capacity of an asset (often referred to as current replacement cost). Fair value is determined based on the cost to a market participant (buyer) to acquire or construct a substitute asset of comparable utility, adjusted for obsolescence.

The fair value of contributed services that create or enhance nonfinancial assets should be estimated based on (a) the fair value of the services received or (b) the fair value of the assets created (or the change in the fair value of the asset that is being enhanced), whichever is more readily determinable. A fair value measurement should be determined based on the assumptions that market participants would use in pricing the asset. Market participant assumptions should include assumptions about the effect of a restriction on the sale or use of an asset if market participants would consider the effect of the restriction in pricing the asset.

FASB ASC 820-10-55-51 *Example 6: Restricted Assets* explains that restrictions that are an attribute of an asset, and therefore would transfer to a market participant, are the only restrictions reflected in fair value. Donor restrictions that are specific to the donee are reflected in the classification of net assets, not in the measurement of fair value.

Major uncertainties about the existence of value of a contributed asset may indicate that a contribution should not be recognized. Such uncertainties are often present when an item has no use other than for scientific or educational research or for its historical significance. Examples of such items include flora, fauna, photographs, and objects identified with historic persons, places, or events.

If a promise to give has not previously been recognized as contribution revenue because it was conditional, fair value should be measured when the conditions are met.

The present value of the future cash flows is one valuation technique for measuring the fair value of contributions arising from unconditional promises to give cash; other valuation techniques also are available, as described in FASB ASC 820. Exhibit 2-5 illustrates the use of present value techniques for initial recognition and measurement of unconditional promises to give cash that are expected to be collected one year or more after the financial statement date.

Appendix A includes excerpts from the AICPA white paper *Measurement of Fair Value for Certain Transactions of Not-for-Profit Entities* that discuss fair value measurement of a promise to give cash and other financial assets that are due in one year or more.

Exhibit 2-5: Initial recognition of unconditional promises to give cash

Facts

Assume that an NFP entity receives a promise (or promises from a group of homogeneous donors) to give $100 in five years, that the anticipated future cash flows from the promise(s) are $70, and that the present value of the future cash flows is $50.

Solution

dr. Contributions Receivable $70
cr. Contribution Revenue — Net assets with donor restrictions $50
cr. Discount on Contributions Receivable $20

(To report contributions receivable and revenue using a present value technique to measure fair value.)

(Note: Some entities may use a subsidiary ledger to retain information concerning the $100 face amount of contributions promised in order to monitor collections of contributions promised.)

A present value technique is one valuation technique for measuring the fair value of an unconditional promise to give noncash assets; other valuation techniques also are available, as described in FASB ASC 820. If present value techniques are used, the fair value of contributions arising from unconditional promises to give noncash assets might be determined based on the present value of the projected fair value of the underlying noncash assets at the date and in the quantities that those assets are expected to be received, if the date is one year or more after the financial statement date. (Both the [a] likelihood of the promise being fulfilled and [b] future fair value of those underlying assets, such as the future fair value per share of a promised equity security, should be considered in determining the future amount to be discounted.) In cases in which the future fair value of the underlying asset is difficult to determine, the fair value of an unconditional promise to give noncash assets may be based on the fair value of the underlying asset at the date of initial recognition. (No discount for the time value of money should be reported if an asset's fair value at the date of initial recognition is used to measure the fair value of the contribution.)

If present value techniques are used to measure the fair value of unconditional promises to give, an NFP entity should determine the amount and timing of the future cash flows of unconditional promises to give cash (or, for promises to give noncash assets, the quantity and nature of assets expected to be received). In making that determination, NFP entities should consider all the elements in FASB ASC 820-10-55-5, including when the receivable is expected to be collected, the creditworthiness of the other parties, the organization's past collection experience and its policies concerning the enforcement of promises to give, expectations about possible variations in the amount or timing of the cash flows (that is, the uncertainty inherent in the cash flows), or both, and other factors concerning the receivable's collectibility.

Identifying gains and losses

We have already addressed several aspects regarding the treatment of gains and losses. Now we will briefly further address the identification of gains and losses. Gains and losses result both from an organization's peripheral or incidental activities and from events and circumstances that stem from the environment and that are largely beyond the control of a particular entity and its management. The following are some examples of activities that may be reported as gains and losses:

- Change in fair value of equity securities
- Losses from natural events, such as fire or floods
- Gains or losses from the sale of land or buildings no longer needed for operations
- Gains or losses from settling a lawsuit

Knowledge check

7. Which is accurate of identifying gains and losses?

    a. Examples of activities that may be reported as gains and losses would include changes in fair value of equity securities.
    b. Whether an item is a revenue or expense, or a gain or loss is not an important determination in financial reporting for NFPs.
    c. An example of something that may be reported as gains and losses would be donations received at an annual fund-raising event.
    d. All gains and losses are reported as net assets without donor restrictions.

Agency transactions

There are several situations in which an NFP entity receives assets it has little discretion over the use of. In these cases, the NFP entity may be acting as an agent, trustee, or intermediary in helping a donor make a contribution to another entity or individual. FASB ASC 958-605 provides guidance on how to report such transactions.

Some examples of entities that receive assets that will be passed to other entities are federated fund-raising entities, community foundations, and institutionally related entities, but any entity can function in those capacities. An example of this type of transaction is a situation in which a donor passes assets to an NFP entity (recipient organization) and instructs that entity to transfer those assets to another entity (the beneficiary) named by the donor.

The donor may specify the beneficiary by

- name.
- stating that all entities that meet a set of donor-defined criteria are beneficiaries.
- actions surrounding the transfer that make clear the identity of the beneficiary.

In general, the recipient entity should not recognize contribution revenue when it receives such assets and should not report a donation when it transfers the assets to the beneficiary. Instead, the recipient entity would record an increase to assets and liabilities for the fair value of assets received. When assets are transferred to the beneficiary, the recipient entity would reduce assets and liabilities.

In some cases, a donor may explicitly grant a recipient entity the unilateral power to redirect (variance power) the transferred assets to an entity other than the beneficiary specified by the donor. When this happens, the recipient entity would recognize contribution revenue for the amount of transferred assets as long as the named beneficiary is unaffiliated with the donor. If the donor names itself or its affiliates, the recipient entity would not recognize contribution revenue.

Summary

NFP entities receive inflows of resources from a variety of sources. The source of the inflows affects how the transactions are measured and reported. Due to the variety of sources, the accounting and reporting for this area can become complex. However, this information is important to financial statement users.

NFPs must first determine whether a transaction is an exchange transaction or a contribution. For exchange transactions, revenue is recognized when an NFP satisfies a performance obligation by transferring a promised good or service to a customer.

For a contribution, the NFP must then determine if it is conditional or unconditional. Revenue is recognized when the contribution becomes unconditional. Contributions can also contain donor-imposed restrictions that will increase net assets with donor restrictions.

Practice questions

1. A donor unconditionally promises to give an NFP museum $1,000 next year to support general operations. How should this promise be reported in the statement of activities?

    a. Not reported until the cash is received.
    b. Deferred revenue.
    c. Revenue that increases net assets without donor restrictions.
    d. Revenue that increases net assets with donor restrictions.

2. An NFP museum has adopted a policy of not capitalizing its collection of works of art. The museum receives a donation of a painting with a fair value of $30,000 that is added to the collection. How should this contribution be reported in the statement of activities?

    a. It would not be reported in the statement of activities.
    b. Revenue that increases net assets with donor restrictions.
    c. Revenue that increases net assets without donor restrictions.
    d. Reported as a gain that increases net assets without donor restrictions.

3. An attorney volunteers 100 hours a year serving meals at an NFP shelter. The attorney's normal billing rate is $50 an hour. What amount of donated services should the shelter report in the statement of activities?

    a. $0.
    b. $1,000.
    c. $2,500.
    d. $5,000.

4. An NFP entity receives a notice that a donor plans to list the entity as a $10,000 beneficiary in her will. How should the entity record this notice in the statement of activities?

    a. Contribution revenue for the net realizable value of the pledge.
    b. Contribution revenue for the face value of the pledge.
    c. No amount of revenue should be reported.

5. For the following items, indicate how the item generally should be reported using one of the following:

    Exchange transaction (E)
    Contribution revenue that increase net assets without donor restrictions (UC)
    Contribution revenue that increase net assets with donor restrictions (RC)
    Not reported in statement of activities (NR)

    _____ Unconditional promises to give with payments due in future periods
    _____ Gift of a car the entity plans to sell
    _____ Dues that cover the cost of publications
    _____ Gift of securities to create an endowment fund
    _____ Gift of art work to a collection (collection not capitalized)
    _____ Donated accounting services by a CPA
    _____ Free use of office space in the current year
    _____ Conditional promise to give if an organization can raise a certain amount
    _____ Donated services to replace a roof

Case study: The Homeless Shelter of the New River Valley

Case study: Background information

The Homeless Shelter of the New River Valley (HSNRV) is a local NFP entity governed by people who volunteer to serve on the board of directors and other committees and teams. The HSNRV is focused on providing temporary shelter to homeless people in the community. The organization receives its annual operating funds from donations made by individuals and businesses in the community.

The HSNRV is governed by a 20-member board of directors. Members of the board receive no compensation for their services. HSNRV has a volunteer treasurer who is appointed to a three-year term. The current treasurer is an accounting faculty member at a nearby state university. She is a CPA.

The HSNRV kicked off their capital campaign to raise money for a new shelter with a special fund-raising event. Catering, promotional materials, and entertainment for the event cost $15,000. The coach of the state university's football team agreed to be the speaker at the event. The coach has been very successful and usually receives a minimum of $5,000 for any speaking engagement. He has agreed to donate his time for this event.

During the event the following unconditional promises to give were received:

- 200 people pledged $100 each to be paid within one year. Based on past experience, the college expects to collect 95% of this amount.
- Twenty people joined the President's Club by pledging $10,000 each to be paid at the end of three years. The college expects to collect 90% ($180,000) of this amount. The college estimates the present value of the $180,000 to be $155,000.

HSNRV has adopted a policy to measure unconditional promises to give expected to be collected within one year at their net realizable value. Other unconditional promises to give are measured using a present value technique.

HSNRV reported the following transactions for the year:

- Donor A contributes $5,000 to purchase new beds for the shelter.
- The HSNRV receives a federal grant of $50,000 to support housing 10 homeless people.
- Donor B promises to contribute $10,000 if the HSNRV increases the number of people served by the shelter by 10% in the coming year.
- The local hardware store enters into an agreement with HSNRV to pay $10 per straw basket made by people staying at the shelter. The fair value of the baskets is $6 each.

Case study: The Homeless Shelter of the New River Valley (continued)

Case study exercise 1

Indicate which contributed services you believe should be recognized. If you believe that the service should be recognized, also indicate how you might value the service.

Item	Should the contributed service be recognized? If the service should be recognized, how might you value the service?
The normal duties of the treasurer	
The football coach's speech	

Case study exercise 2

Review the questions listed in the following chart related to HSNRV. Use the right column to answer each question.

Question	Answer
How would you prepare the journal entry for the 200 people who pledged $100 each to be paid within one year?	
How would you prepare the journal entry for the 20 people who pledged $10,000 each to be paid in three years?	

Case study: The Homeless Shelter of the New River Valley (continued)

Case study exercise 3

How should the following transactions be reported (unconditional contribution, conditional contribution, or exchange transaction)? Also indicate whether the transaction would increase net assets with donor restrictions. Use the right column to answer each question.

Transaction	Answer
Donor A contributes $5,000 to purchase new beds for the shelter.	
The HSNRV receives a federal grant of $50,000 to support housing 10 homeless people.	
Donor B promises to contribute $10,000 if the HSNRV increases the number of people served by the shelter by 10% in the coming year.	
The local hardware store enters into an agreement with HSNRV to pay $10 per straw basket made by people staying at the shelter. The fair value of the baskets is $6 each.	

Chapter 3

Expenses

Learning objectives

- Identify how to report an analysis of expenses by function and nature.

- Identify the criteria used to determine whether joint costs can be allocated.

- Identify how to report reclassifications.

Introduction

Prior to the implementation of Accounting Standards Update (ASU) No. 2016-14, *Presentation of Financial Statements of Not-for-Profit Entities*, there were inconsistencies in the types of information provided about expenses — for example, some, but not all, not-for-profits (NFPs) provided information about expenses by both nature and function. Also, only certain types of NFPs (voluntary health and welfare organizations) were required to include a statement of functional expenses. Now, all NFPs are to report amounts of expenses by both their natural classification and their functional classifications in one location, on the face of the statement of activities, as a separate statement, or in the notes to financial statements.

Expenses versus losses

An important determination in financial reporting for NFPs is whether an item is an expense or a loss. Consider the differences between expenses and losses:

- *Expenses* are outflows of or other ways of using up assets or incurrences of liabilities (or a combination of both) from delivering or producing goods, rendering services, or carrying out other activities that constitute the entity's ongoing major or central operations.
- *Losses* are different from expenses. Losses result from activities that are peripheral or incidental to the organization. Activities that are reported as expenses by some entities may be reported as losses by others. It will depend on whether the activity is part of the organization's ongoing major or central operations.

The determination is important because of the following:

- *There are differences in how expenses and losses are reported.* Expenses are reported gross, except investment expenses, where losses may be reported net.
- *Expenses are always reported as decreases in net assets without donor restrictions.*
- *NFP entities are required to report information about the functional and natural classification of expenses, such as major classes of program services and supporting activities.* This information can be done on the face of the statement of activities, as a separate statement or in the notes to the financial statements. Losses need not be reported by a functional classification or in the matrix that presents information about expenses according to both their functional and natural classifications.

Again, activities that are reported as expenses by some entities may be reported as losses by others. For example, a Girl Scouts council could have an annual cookie sale that is its main fund-raising event each year (a major and central activity), whereas a Boy Scouts council could hold a special fund-raising cookie sale for new camping equipment that may be considered a peripheral or incidental activity. Both groups are selling cookies but their reporting of the activity is potentially different.

Special events and other fund-raising activities

Many entities have fund-raising or other special events in which the attendee receives some type of direct benefit. For example, an entity may hold a $100 per plate special dinner as a fund-raising event. An entity may also hold special social or educational events where the attendee receives a direct benefit. Often, these activities are considered part of the organization's ongoing and major activities and therefore revenues and expenses from such events must be reported separately.

Entities have several ways they can report the revenues and expenses from these types of activities. The following is an example of the different ways entities can report a special fund-raising dinner in the statement of activities. Assume the following:

- The price of the dinner is $100.
- The cost of the dinner is $25.
- The fair value of the dinner is $30.
- Additional costs incurred with promoting the dinner are $10.

Now, let us review the possible reporting of this in exhibit 3-1.

Exhibit 3-1: Three examples of reporting a special fund-raising dinner

Example 1

Contributions		$ 0
Special event revenue	100	
Less: Cost of direct benefits to donors	(25)	
Net revenue from special events		75
Total contributions and net revenue		75
Fund-raising expense		10
Increase in net assets without donor restrictions		$ 65

Example 2

Contributions	$ 0
Special event revenue	100
Total revenue	100
Cost of direct benefits to donors	25
Fund-raising expenses	10
Total expenses	35
Increase in net assets without donor restrictions	$ 65

Example 3

Contributions		$ 70
Dinner sales	30	
Less: Cost of direct benefits to donors	(25)	
Gross profit on special events		5
Total contributions and net revenue		75
Fund-raising expenses		10
Increase in net assets without donor restrictions		$ 65

Important point

These three examples assume that the special event is part of the organization's ongoing major or central operations and therefore the revenues and expenses from such events are reported gross. If the special event is peripheral or incidental, the entity is permitted to report the activity net of related direct costs.

Functional reporting of expenses

NFP entities are required to report information about the nature and function of expenses. Functional expense classification is a method of grouping expenses according to the purpose for which costs are incurred, such as major classes of program services and supporting activities. This information can be presented in the statement of activities, as a separate statement, or in the notes to the financial statements.

> Program services are activities that result in goods and services being distributed to beneficiaries, customers, or members that fulfill the purposes or mission of the organization. Supporting services are activities other than program services and include management and general, fund-raising, and membership-development activities. Supporting services may include, as one or more separate categories, cost of sales and costs of other revenue-generating activities that are not program-related.

The proper classification of expenses between program services and supporting services is often important to NFP entities. Resource providers often compare the percentage of expenses that go to providing program services to the percentage of expenses that go to supporting services. Ideally, most of the resources provided to an entity will be used for program services.

Knowledge check

1. Which is accurate of the functional reporting of expenses?

    a. Program services are not activities that result in goods and services being distributed to beneficiaries, customers, or members that fulfill the purposes or mission of the organization.
    b. Supporting services may not include, as one or more separate categories, cost of sales and costs of other revenue-generating activities that are not program-related.
    c. Supporting services are activities other than program services and include management and general, fund-raising, and membership-development activities.
    d. Classification of supporting services other than management and general and fund-raising cannot be used by entities.

2. Which is accurate of the functional reporting of expenses?

    a. The proper classification of expenses between program services and supporting services is often important to NFP entities.
    b. An entity cannot report expense information about program services that it provides.
    c. Resource providers rarely compare the percentage of expenses that go to providing program services to the percentage of expenses that go to supporting services.
    d. Functional reporting of expenses must be reported in the statement of activities.

Program services

An entity must report expense information about program services that it provides. The relationship between functional classification and natural classification for all expenses shall be presented in an analysis that disaggregates functional expense classifications, such as major classes of program services and supporting activities by their natural expense classifications. The financial statements shall provide a description of the nature of the NFP's activities, including a description of each of its major classes of programs. If not provided in the notes to the financial statements, the description can be presented on the statement of activities (for example, using column headings).

For example, a college may report student instruction, research, public service, and other program areas. An entity should report information for each of its major classes of program services and supporting activities. The number of classes to use requires professional judgment. Entities may consider guidance in FASB *Accounting Standards Codification* (ASC) 280-10-50 in determining the number of major classes to use.

Knowledge check

3. Which is accurate of reporting expense information about program services?

    a. All entities may only report a single classification of program expenses.
    b. Entities cannot consider guidance in FASB ASC 280 in determining the number of major classes to use.
    c. Professional judgment is required when determining the number of classes of major programs.
    d. Entities may not report more than five program service classifications.

Supporting services

Supporting services are often classified as management and general, fund-raising, and membership development. However, some NFP industries use other classifications of supporting services. For example, most colleges report institutional support and institutional development activities. Entities may also report more detailed classifications for each type of supporting services.

Management and general activities typically include all items not reported as program services, fund-raising, or membership development. Examples of management and general activities are illustrated as follows:

- Oversight
- Business management
- General record keeping and payroll
- Budgeting
- Financing
- Soliciting revenue from exchange transactions

- Administering government, foundation, and similar customer-sponsored contracts, including billing and collecting fees and grant and contract financial reporting
- Disseminating information to inform the public of the NFP's stewardship of contributed funds
- Making announcements concerning appointments
- Producing and disseminating the annual report
- All management and administration except for direct conduct of program services or fund-raising activities

The cost of oversight and management usually includes the salaries and expenses of the governing board, the chief executive officer, and the supporting staff. If such staff spend a portion of their time directly conducting or supervising program services or categories of other supporting services, however, their salaries and expenses should be allocated among those functions.

Fund-raising activities are connected with inducing potential donors to contribute. The contribution can be money, other assets of value, services, facilities, or time. The activities include

- publicizing and conducting fund-raising events;
- maintaining donor mailing lists;
- conducting special fund-raising events;
- preparing and distributing fund-raising manuals, instructions, and other materials; and
- other activities connected with soliciting contributions from individuals, foundations, governments, and others.

The financial statements should disclose total fund-raising expenses. It should also be noted that fund-raising costs should be expensed as incurred. However, the costs of tangible fund-raising assets, such as brochures and promotional items, may be recorded as assets upon purchase and expensed when used.

In some cases, fund-raising activities are conducted by professional fundraisers or federated fund-raising entities on behalf of an NFP organization. For example, the professional fundraiser may charge a 20% fee for conducting a fund-raising activity, or a federated fund-raising entity may charge a 5% administrative fee for gifts that will be transferred to the NFP organization. In such cases, the NFP should report the gross amount of the contributions raised and a fund-raising expense for any fee.

Membership-development activities include soliciting for prospective members and membership dues, membership relations, and similar activities. To the extent that member benefits are received, membership is an exchange (reciprocal) transaction. If there are no significant benefits or duties connected with membership, however, the substance of membership-development activities may, in fact, be fund-raising, and the related costs should be reported as fund-raising costs.

Membership-development activities may be conducted in conjunction with other activities. In circumstances in which membership development is in part soliciting revenues from exchange (reciprocal) transactions and in part soliciting contributions, the activity is a joint activity. If membership development is a joint activity and the purpose, audience, and content of the activity are appropriate for achieving membership development, joint costs should be allocated between fund-raising and the exchange transaction. In circumstances in which membership development is conducted in conjunction with other activities but does not include soliciting contributions, the activity is not a joint activity, and the costs should be allocated to membership development and one or more other functions. For example, membership may entitle the members to group life and other insurance at reduced costs because of the organization's negotiated rates and to a subscription to the organization's magazine or newsletter. Under these circumstances, an appropriate part of the costs of soliciting members should be allocated to the membership-development function and a part to program services.

Costs related to sales of goods and services that are related to major or central activity of an entity should be reported separately. Cost of sales and services is permitted to be reported immediately after revenue from the sale of merchandise. If the sale of merchandise is related to the organization's mission, the cost of sales could be reported as a program expense. For example, if a museum has a store that sells merchandise related to the museum's program, the cost of the store's sales could be reported as a program expense. If the sale of merchandise is not related to the organization's mission, cost of sales would be reported as supporting services.

Knowledge check

4. Which is accurate of management and general activities?

    a. They exclude budgeting activities.
    b. They exclude oversight activities.
    c. They include financing activities.
    d. They include fund-raising activities.

Analysis of expense by nature and function

All NFPs shall report information about all expenses by function and nature in one location — on the face of the statement of activities, as a schedule in the notes to financial statements, or in a separate financial statement.

All expenses shall be presented in an analysis that disaggregates functional expense classifications, such as major classes of program services and supporting activities by their natural expense classifications, such as salaries, rent, electricity, supplies, interest expense, depreciation, awards and grants to others, and professional fees. Expenses reported in cost of goods sold or services provided (or costs related to special events) should be reported by their natural classification in the functional expense analysis. For example, salaries, wages, and fringe benefits that are included as part of the cost of goods sold on the statement of activities shall be included with other salaries, wages, and fringe benefits in the functional expense analysis.

Exhibit 3-2 is a simple example using a statement of functional expenses:

Exhibit 3-2

Not-for-Profit "D"
Statement of Functional Expenses
Year Ended December 31, 20X8
(in thousands)

	Program	Management and General	Fund-raising	Total
		Supporting Services		
Awards and grants	$50,632	$ —	$ —	$ 50,632
Salaries	2,720	9,471	12,076	24,267
Employee benefits	365	1,717	8,466	10,548
Payroll taxes	145	2,132	1,680	3,957
Professional fees	142	1,096	1,338	2,576
Supplies	72	628	1,618	2,318
Telephone	191	562	1,206	1,959
Postage and shipping	44	416	2,929	3,389
Occupancy	287	1,695	2,591	4,573
Information processing	656	562	1,549	2,767
Printing and publications	135	612	4,885	5,632
Meetings and conferences	719	1,085	2,167	3,971
Other travel	191	788	1,192	2,171
Other expenses	159	919	502	1,580
Depreciation	634	913	1,534	3,081
Total expenses	$ 57,092	$ 22,596	$ 43,733	$123,421

Knowledge check

5. Which is accurate of analysis expenses by function and nature?

    a. The analysis is required for all NFP entities.
    b. The analysis reports expenses by natural classification only.
    c. It is only required for voluntary health and welfare entities.
    d. The analysis is optional for all NFP entities.

Classification of expenses related to more than one function

As stated earlier, the proper classification of expenses between program services and supporting activities is often important to NFP entities. Some expenses are easily assigned to a single program or supporting activity. However, some expenses relate to more than one program or supporting activity and must be allocated to the appropriate functions. For example, rent on a building may need to be allocated among program services and supporting activities.

Where possible, direct identification of specific expense is the preferable method of charging expenses to various functions. For example, travel costs incurred in connection with a program activity should be assigned to that program.

Often, it may not be possible or practical to use direct identification to assign costs to various functions. In such cases, an allocation method would be used. Allocating costs is a common practice for both NFP entities and business enterprises. A reasonable allocation of expenses can be made in a variety of ways and should be based on an objective method.

Allocation methods may be based on financial or nonfinancial data. For example, building costs (rent and utilities) may be allocated based on square footage of space occupied by the various programs and support activities. Time records or activity reports may be used to allocate salary of certain personnel. Entities should review their allocation methods periodically to ensure they reflect the most current activity. A description of the methods used to allocate costs among program and support functions would need to be disclosed in the notes to the financial statements.

There is special guidance on allocating costs related to an activity that combines fund-raising activities and also elements of another function. These types of costs are referred to as *joint activities* and are discussed in the next section.

Expenses of materials and activities that combine fund-raising activities with activities that have elements of another function (joint activities)

NFP entities may solicit support through a variety of fund-raising activities, including the following:

- Direct mail
- Telephone solicitation
- Door-to-door canvassing
- Telethons
- Special events
- Other similar activities

Sometimes fund-raising activities are conducted with activities related to other functions, such as program activities or supporting services, such as management and general activities. Sometimes fund-raising activities include components that would otherwise be associated with program or supporting services, but in fact support fund-raising.

> If the following criteria of purpose, audience, and content are met, the costs of a joint activity that are identifiable with a particular function should be charged to that function and joint costs should be allocated between fund-raising and the appropriate program or management and general function.

If any of the criteria are not met, all costs of the joint activity should be reported as fund-raising costs, including costs that otherwise might be considered program or management and general costs if they had been incurred in a different activity, subject to the following exception. Costs of goods or services provided in exchange transactions that are part of joint activities, such as costs of direct donor benefits of a special event (for example, a meal), should not be reported as fund-raising.

Purpose

The purpose criterion is met if the purpose of the joint activity includes accomplishing program or management and general functions.

Program functions

To accomplish program functions, the activity would call for specific action by the audience that will help accomplish the organization's mission. For example, an entity with a mission to get people to stop smoking may send a brochure that urges the recipient to stop smoking and provides methods to accomplish this task.

One may wonder whether asking an audience to make contributions is a call for specific action. Asking an audience to make contributions is not a call for specific action by the audience that will help accomplish the organization's mission.

Program and management and general functions

The following factors should be considered to determine if the purpose criterion is met:

1. *Whether compensation or fees for performing the activity are based on contributions raised.* The purpose criterion is not met if a majority of compensation or fees for any party's performance of any component of the discrete joint activity varies based on contributions raised for that discrete joint activity.
2. *Whether a similar program or management and general activity is conducted separately and on a similar or greater scale.* (Note: If the purpose criterion is met based on the factor in the final bullet that follows, "other evidence" should not be considered.) The purpose criterion is met if either of the following two conditions is met:

a. *Condition 1.* The program component of the joint activity calls for specific action by the recipient that will help accomplish the organization's mission and a similar program component is conducted without the fund-raising component using the same medium and on a scale that is similar to or greater than the scale on which it is conducted with the fund-raising.

b. *Condition 2.* A management and general activity that is similar to the management and general component of the joint activity being accounted for is conducted without the fund-raising component using the same medium and on a scale that is similar to or greater than the scale on which it is conducted with the fund-raising.

3. *Other evidence.* If the factors discussed previously do not determine whether the purpose criterion is met, other evidence may determine whether the criterion is met. All available evidence, both positive and negative, should be considered to determine whether, based on the weight of that evidence, the purpose criterion is met.

Audience

A rebuttable presumption exists that the audience criterion is not met if the audience includes prior donors or is otherwise selected based on its ability or likelihood to contribute to the organization. That presumption can be overcome if the audience is also selected for one or more of the reasons listed subsequently. In determining whether that presumption is overcome, entities should consider the extent to which the audience is selected based on its ability or likelihood to contribute to the entity and contrast that with the extent to which it is selected for one or more of the reasons listed subsequently. For example, if the audience's ability or likelihood to contribute is a significant factor in its selection and it has a need for the action related to the program component of the joint activity, but having that need is an insignificant factor in its selection, the presumption would not be overcome.

In circumstances in which the audience includes no prior donors and is not otherwise selected based on its ability or likelihood to contribute to the organization, the audience criterion is met if the audience is selected for one or more of the following reasons:

- The audience's need to use or reasonable potential for use of the specific action called for by the program component of the joint activity.
- The audience's ability to take specific action to assist the entity in meeting the goals of the program component of the joint activity.
- The entity is required to direct the management and general component of the joint activity to the particular audience or the audience has reasonable potential for use of the management and general component.

Content

The content criterion is met if the joint activity supports program or management and general functions, as follows:

- *Program.* The joint activity calls for specific action by the recipient that will help accomplish the organization's mission. If the need for and benefits of the action are not clearly evident, information describing the action and explaining the need for and benefits of the action is provided.
- *Management and general.* The joint activity fulfills one or more of the organization's management and general responsibilities through a component of the joint activity.

Information identifying and describing the organization, causes, or how the contributions provided will be used is considered in support of fund-raising.

Charting the process

As we have just described, the process for accounting for joint activities is complex. Exhibit 3-3 illustrates how to apply the criteria of purpose, audience, and content.

In the preceding discussion we have attempted to summarize and simplify a rather complicated subject. For important details on this topic see FASB ASC 958-605, which is available at www.fasb.org.

Exhibit 3-3: Accounting for joint activities[1]

The following flowchart from FASB ASC 958-720-55-2 summarizes the guidance in paragraphs 29–53 of FASB ASC 958-720-45 (see paragraphs 13.90–.126 in the AICPA Audit and Accounting Guide *Not-for-Profit Entities*) and is not intended as a substitute for the guidance therein.

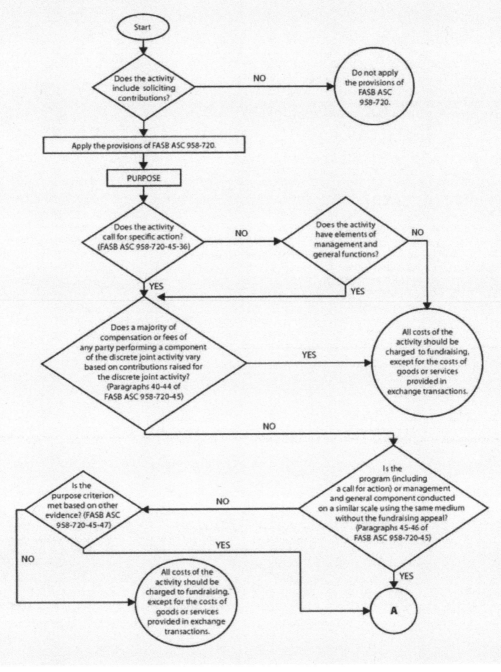

[1] From AICPA Audit and Accounting Guide Not-for-Profit Entities. ©2018, AICPA. All rights reserved. This product is available at www.aicpastore.com.

Exhibit 3-3: Accounting for joint activities (continued)

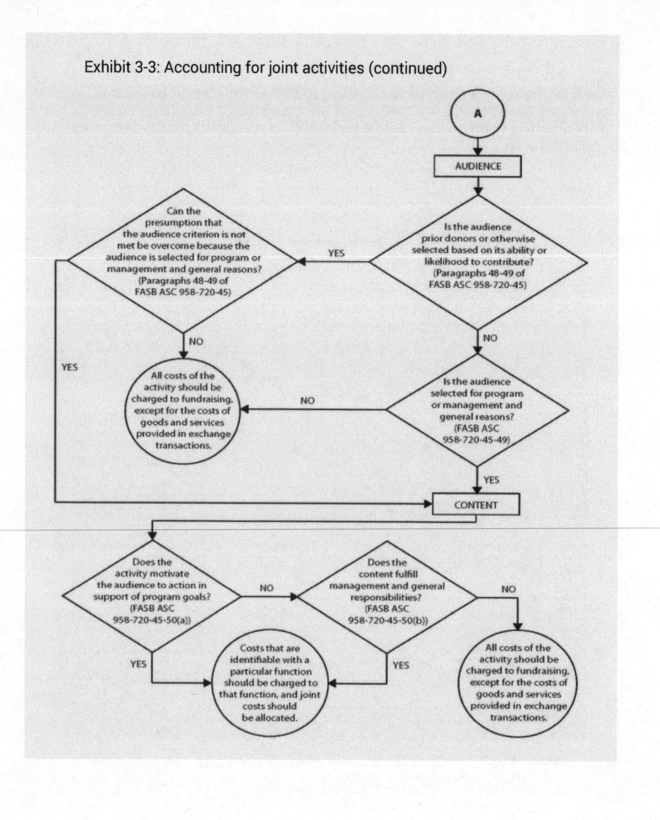

A

AUDIENCE

Is the audience prior donors or otherwise selected based on its ability or likelihood to contribute? (Paragraphs 48-49 of FASB ASC 958-720-45)

YES →

Can the presumption that the audience criterion is not met be overcome because the audience is selected for program or management and general reasons? (Paragraphs 48-49 of FASB ASC 958-720-45)

NO

All costs of the activity should be charged to fundraising, except for the costs of goods and services provided in exchange transactions.

YES

NO (from audience prior donors)

Is the audience selected for program or management and general reasons? (FASB ASC 958-720-45-49)

NO →

YES

CONTENT

Does the activity motivate the audience to action in support of program goals? (FASB ASC 958-720-45-50(a))

NO →

Does the content fulfill management and general responsibilities? (FASB ASC 958-720-45-50(b))

NO →

All costs of the activity should be charged to fundraising, except for the costs of goods and services provided in exchange transactions.

YES (from motivate)

Costs that are identifiable with a particular function should be charged to that function, and joint costs should be allocated.

YES (from content fulfill)

Allocation methods

The cost allocation method used should be rational and systematic, it should result in an allocation of joint costs that is reasonable, and it should be applied consistently given similar facts and circumstances.

Disclosures

As illustrated in the following, NFPs that allocate joint costs have several disclosure requirements.

> NFPs that allocate joint costs should disclose
> the following in the notes to their financial statements:
>
> - The types of activities for which joint costs have been incurred
> - A statement that such costs have been allocated
> - The total amount allocated during the period and the portion allocated to each functional expense category

Entities are encouraged, but not required, to disclose the amount of joint costs for each kind of joint activity, if practical.

Have we covered everything regarding joint activities?

We have had a lengthy discussion of joint activities and one may wonder at this point if we have covered everything. In a word, no, but we have covered the core requirements and issues. For more information on this topic, consult chapter 13 of AICPA Audit and Accounting Guide *Not-for-Profit Entities*.

Reclassifications

Some contributions are limited by donor-imposed stipulations that either expire by passage of time (time restriction) or can be fulfilled and removed by actions of the entity pursuant to these stipulations (purpose restriction).

The expiration of a donor-imposed restriction simultaneously increases net assets without donor restrictions and decreases net assets with donor restrictions and is referred to as a reclassification. Reclassifications are reported as separate items in the statement of activities. For example, a donor contributes $1,000 to cover the cost of a training program for staff of an NFP organization. The entity can meet this restriction by spending the $1,000 on the training program. The cost of the program would be reported as an expense that decreases net assets without donor restrictions and a reclassification would be reported that simultaneously increases net assets without donor restrictions and decreases net assets with donor restrictions.

Reclassifications of net assets should be made if

- the entity fulfills the purposes for which the net assets were restricted;
- donor-imposed restrictions expire with the passage of time or with the death of a split-interest agreement beneficiary (if the net assets are not otherwise restricted);
- a donor withdraws, or court action removes, previously imposed restrictions; or
- donors impose restrictions on otherwise net assets without donor restrictions.

Expenses may be incurred for purposes for which both non-donor restricted and donor restricted net assets are available. If an expense is incurred for a purpose for which both net assets with and without donor restrictions are available, a donor-imposed restriction is fulfilled to the extent of the expense incurred unless the expense is for a purpose that is directly attributable to another specific external source of revenue. For example, an employee's salary may meet donor-imposed restrictions to support the program on which the employee is working. In that situation, the restriction is met to the extent of the salary expense incurred unless incurring the salary will lead to inflows of revenues from a specific external source, such as revenues from a cost reimbursement contract or a conditional promise to give that becomes unconditional when the entity incurs the salary expense.

An entity may meet donor-imposed restrictions on all or a portion of the amount contributed in the same reporting period in which the contribution is received. NFP entities can adopt an accounting policy were the contribution (to the extent that the restrictions have been met) would be reported as an increase in net assets without donor restrictions. The entity must have a similar policy for reporting investment gains and income, reports consistently from period to period, and discloses its accounting policy in the notes to the financial statements. This is illustrated in exhibit 3-4.

Exhibit 3-4: Satisfying donor-imposed restrictions in the period received

Assume that Entities A and B each received $100,000 contributions that were restricted for supporting after school programs. Also assume that both entities incurred $100,000 in expenses related to the after school programs in the same year that the restricted contributions were received. Entity A has a policy of recording such contributions as net assets without donor restrictions. However, Entity B does not. The following illustrates the effects of these decisions on line items within the statement of activities.

	Net assets without donor restrictions	Net assets with donor restrictions
Entity A		
Contributions	$100,000	$—
Program expenses	−100,000	
Change in net assets	—	—
Entity B		
Contributions	$—	$100,000
Net assets released from restriction	100,000	−100,000
Program expenses	−100,000	
Change in net assets	—	—

Summary

NFP entities are required to report expenses gross, where gains and losses may be reported net. In addition, expenses are always reported as decreases in net assets without donor restrictions. Gains and losses may change the other class of net assets if the use of such gains and losses is restricted by a donor or law.

NFP entities are required to report information about the nature and functional classification of expenses, such as major classes of program services and supporting activities. This information can be presented on the face of the statement of activities, as a separate statement, or in the notes to the financial statements.

The proper classification of expenses between program services and supporting activities is often important to NFP entities. There are special rules for allocation costs of an activity that combines fund-raising activities with activities that have elements of another function (joint activities).

The expiration of the donor-imposed restriction simultaneously increases net assets without donor restrictions and decreases net assets with donor restrictions (reclassifications) which are reported as separate items in the statement of activities.

Practice questions

1. Which is accurate of expenses?

   a. Expenses are outflows of assets or incurrences of liabilities that result from an organization's ongoing major or central operations and activities.
   b. Expenses are decreases in net assets from an organization's peripheral or incidental transactions.
   c. Expenses must be reported net.
   d. None of the above.

2. Which is accurate of supporting activities?

   a. Supporting activities do not include fund-raising activities.
   b. Industries cannot have functional categories of supporting activities that are prevalent in that industry.
   c. NFP entities may have various kinds of supporting activities, such as management and general, fund-raising, and membership development.
   d. None of the above.

3. Which is accurate regarding the allocation of expenses?
   a. If an allocation is impossible or impracticable, direct identification is appropriate.
   b. Direct identification of specific expense is the preferable method of charging expenses to various functions.
   c. Subjective methods of allocating expenses are preferable to objective methods.
   d. None of the above.

Case study: The Homeless Shelter of the New River Valley

Case study: Background information

The Homeless Shelter of the New River Valley (HSNRV) is a local not-for-profit entity governed by people who volunteer to serve on the board of directors and other committees and teams. The HSNRV is focused on providing temporary shelter to homeless people in the community. The origination receives its annual operating funds from donations made by individuals and businesses in the community.

The HSNRV is governed by a 20-member board of directors. Members of the board receive no compensation for their services. HSNRV has a volunteer treasurer who is appointed to a three-year term. The current treasurer is an accounting faculty member at a nearby state university. She is a CPA.

The HSNRV kicked off their annual fund-raising event. Catering and entertainment for the event cost $15,000. Promotional costs were $5,000. The fee to attend the event was $100. The fair value of attending the event is estimated to be $15. HSNRV received $85,000 from fees for the event.

HSNRV also reported the following expenses for the year:

- President's salary: $45,000 (The president spends 40% of her time counseling people in the shelter.
- Shelter workers: $40,000 (cleaning and preparing meals)
- Shelter utilities and supplies: $15,000
- Bookkeeper: $10,000
- Annual audit fee and report: $4,000
- Annual fund-raising letters: $5,000

Case study: The Homeless Shelter of the New River Valley (continued)

How should the following expenses be reported by functional classification (program activities, management and general activities, or fund-raising activities)? Use the right column to answer each question.

Expense	Answer
Catering and entertainment for the special fund-raising event cost $15,000	
Promotional costs of $5,000 for the special fund-raising event	
President's salary $45,000 (president spends 40% of her time counseling people in the shelter)	
Shelter workers $40,000 (cleaning and preparing meals)	
Shelter utilities and supplies $15,000	
Bookkeeper $10,000	
Annual audit fee and report $4,000	
Annual fund-raising letters $5,000	

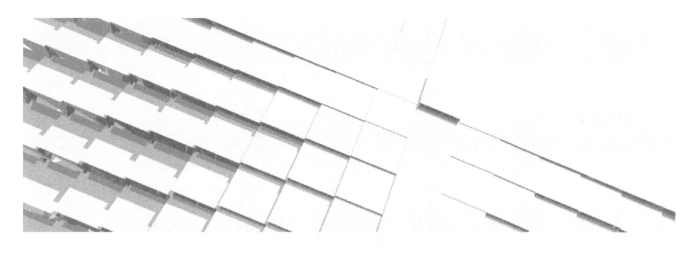

Chapter 4

The Not-for-Profit Environment and Performance Measures

Learning objectives

- Identify the unique aspects of the not-for-profit (NFP) environment.

- Identify the unique accounting and reporting practices used by NFP entities.

- Identify tools available to NFP entities to measure performance.

- Identify measures used related to an organization's service efforts and accomplishments.

Introduction

NFPs are different from for-profit entities in many ways. This chapter will explore the areas that make NFPs unique. It will also discuss how to report and evaluate an NFP, including using ratios and other evaluation tools.

The NFP environment

Key differences

What makes NFP entities different from normal businesses? Well, there are several things. There are environmental factors related to NFP entities that are different, in a number of ways, from businesses. These differences result in different financial reporting objectives and different financial reporting for NFP entities.

FASB identified three key characteristics of an NFP entity in the FASB *Accounting Standards Codification* (ASC) glossary. These characteristics are illustrated in exhibit 4-1.

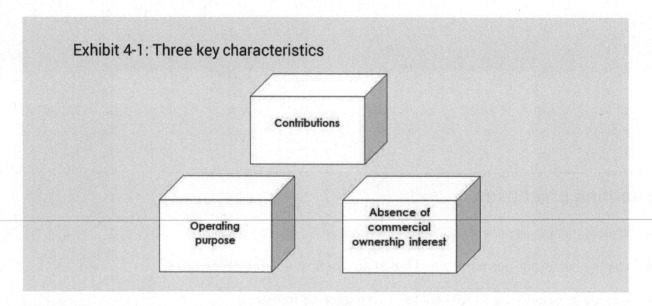

Exhibit 4-1: Three key characteristics

Now let us look at these three major characteristics further:

- *Contributions of significant amounts of resources from resource providers who do not expect commensurate or proportionate pecuniary return (nonreciprocal)*. Businesses are not likely to receive donations and grants from individuals, foundations, governments, or other businesses. Many NFP entities depend on donations and grants as a major source of their operational funding. There are several accounting and reporting issues related to contributions (nonreciprocal transactions).
- *Operating purposes other than to provide goods or services at a profit*. Businesses are in the business of making money. Many of the services NFP entities provide do not have a direct relationship to how much the recipient pays. For example, a local homeless shelter may be supported by contributions, not by charges to the people who actually use the shelter.
- *Absence of ownership interests like those of business entities*. Most NFP entities have no stockholders or owners. They are often governed by self-perpetuating boards, which are often made up of volunteers.

There are other characteristics of NFP entities, but these are the three key characteristics that FASB identified. These characteristics can be present in an entity in varying degrees, and an NFP entity does not have to have all three. For example, an NFP school may not receive any contributions (nonreciprocal transactions) but may rely for its revenue on fees charged to students.

For the most part, NFP entities enter into many of the same transactions that businesses have. For example, NFP entities have payrolls, buy supplies, sell goods, and do many of the same things that business entities do. In general, accounting and reporting for these types of transactions are accounted and reported the same way for both types of entities.

So why are there accounting and financial reporting differences for NFP entities? To a large extent, it is due to the three aforementioned characteristic differences.

Knowledge check

1. Which is accurate of NFP entities?

    a. Many of the services NFP entities provide do not have a direct relationship to how much the recipient pays.
    b. There are no accounting and reporting issues related to contributions.
    c. Few NFP entities depend on donations and grants as a major source of their operational funding.
    d. NFP entities do not enter into many of the same transactions as businesses.

Unique financial reporting objectives

As illustrated in the following, differences in the environment factors result in NFP entities having unique financial reporting objectives:

> FASB Statement of Financial Accounting Concepts No. 4, *Objectives of Financial Reporting by Nonbusiness Organizations*, states that NFP organizations should provide information that is useful to present and future resource providers in
>
> - making rational decisions about the allocation of resources to those organizations.
> - assessing the services that the entity provides and its ability to continue to provide those services.
> - assessing how managers have discharged their stewardship responsibilities and other aspects of their performance.
>
> The financial reports should also provide information about economic resources, obligations, net resources, cash, and changes in these items.

Notice that these objectives are different from those of a business. Determining profitability and net income are not part of the objectives for NFP organizations.

Knowledge check

2. Which is accurate of the financial reporting objectives of NFPs?

    a. Differences in the environment factors result in NFP organizations having unique financial reporting objectives.

    b. NFP reporting objectives are not different from those of a business.

    c. NFP organizations need not provide information that is useful to present or future resource providers in making rational decisions about the allocation of resources to those organizations.

    d. Profitability is a key reporting objective of NFP organizations.

3. Which is accurate of the financial reporting objectives of NFPs?

    a. NFP organizations should not provide information that is useful to present or future resource providers in assessing the services that the entity provides or its ability to continue to provide those services.

    b. Determining profitability and net income are part of the objectives for NFP organizations.

    c. NFP organizations should provide information that is useful to present and future resource providers in assessing how managers have discharged their stewardship responsibilities and other aspects of their performance.

    d. Unique accounting and reporting practices are not needed by NFP organizations to meet financial reporting objectives.

Unique accounting and reporting practices

Because of the special environmental factors and the need to meet the financial reporting objectives stated earlier, several unique accounting and financial reporting practices have evolved for NFP organizations. For the most part, accounting methods used by NFP organizations are the same as those used by businesses. Debits and credits, journals, and ledgers are still used, and many transactions are recorded in the same manner as a business.

However, as illustrated in the following, there are a few major accounting and financial reporting differences and unique transactions for NFP organizations that need to be understood.

Unique NFP accounting and reporting practices

- *Contributions (nonreciprocal transactions).* NFP organizations often receive substantial amounts of donations and grants. Recording and reporting nonreciprocal transactions provides a unique challenge for NFP organizations. In addition, many donations and grants contain restrictions (time or purpose) and other conditions that must be reported and disclosed.
- *Net assets.* What do we call the difference between assets and liabilities? For business, it is often referred to as "stockholder's equity." For an NFP organization, it is called "net assets." In addition, net assets are further divided between net assets without donor restrictions and net assets with donor restrictions.[1]
- *Financial statements.* Because the financial reporting objectives are different for NFP organizations, the financial statements are somewhat different from those of a business. The three general-purpose financial statements for an NFP entity are the statement of financial position, the statement of activities, and the statement of cash flows. All NFP organizations must also present an analysis of expenses by function and nature in one location. This may be presented in the notes to the financial statements, in the statement of activities, or as a separate statement.

---

[1] Prior to ASU No. 2016-14, NFP organizations reported three net asset classes (unrestricted, temporarily restricted, and permanently restricted). For more information, see the discussion later in this chapter and fasb.org.

Types of NFP organizations

FASB ASC and NFP organizations

Because FASB ASC 958 contains incremental industry-specific guidance specifically for NFP organizations, it is important to be clear about which organizations must follow the industry-specific guidance.

In addition to the three characteristics listed earlier that are typically present in NFPs (contributions, operating purpose, and absence of commercial ownership interest), FASB ASC also discusses entities that fall outside the definition of an NFP organization. Organizations excluded are

- all investor-owned entities.
- entities that provide dividends, lower costs, or other economic benefits directly and proportionately to their owners, members, or participants, such as mutual insurance entities, credit unions, farm and rural electric cooperatives, and employee benefit plans.

FASB ASC 958-10-15-3 provides the following list of nongovernmental NFP entities that should apply the incremental industry-specific guidance included in FASB ASC:

- Cemetery organizations
- Civic and community organizations
- Colleges and universities
- Elementary and secondary schools
- Federated fund-raising organizations
- Fraternal organizations
- Health care entities (see following discussion)
- Labor unions
- Libraries
- Museums
- Other cultural organizations
- Performing arts organizations
- Political parties
- Political action committees
- Private and community foundations
- Professional associations
- Public broadcasting stations
- Religious organizations
- Research and scientific organizations
- Social and country clubs
- Trade associations
- Voluntary health and welfare entities
- Zoological and botanical societies

The list is not intended to be all-inclusive. Other entities, if they meet the definition of an NFP entity under FASB ASC, should also follow the incremental industry-specific guidance. It is important to note that additional incremental industry-specific guidance exists for not-for-profit, business-oriented health care entities (see FASB ASC 954).

GASB sets financial reporting standards for governments. It is easy to tell that a city or county is a government, but what about a library or museum? Entities that meet at least one of the following criteria are considered governmental and would follow GASB standards:

- Officers of the entity are popularly elected.
- A controlling majority of the members of the entity's governing board is appointed (or approved) by officials of at least one state or local government.
- A government is able to unilaterally dissolve the entity, with the entity's net assets reverting to a government.
- The entity has the power to enact and enforce a tax levy.
- The entity has the ability to directly issue federally tax-exempt debt.

If the only criterion met is the ability to directly issue federally tax-exempt debt, the presumption that an entity is governmental may be rebutted based on compelling, relevant evidence.

So it should now be clearer which organizations must follow the incremental industry-specific guidance included in the not-for-profit entities topic of FASB ASC (FASB ASC 958). Exhibit 4-2 illustrates what we have discussed.

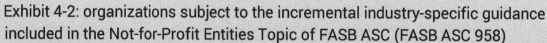

Exhibit 4-2: organizations subject to the incremental industry-specific guidance included in the Not-for-Profit Entities Topic of FASB ASC (FASB ASC 958)

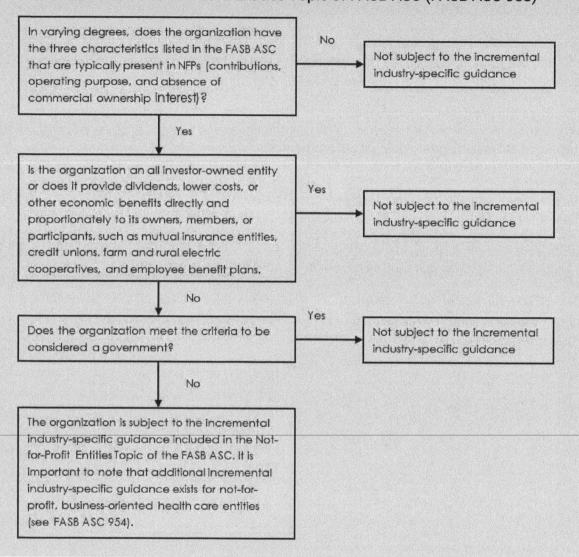

In varying degrees, does the organization have the three characteristics listed in the FASB ASC that are typically present in NFPs (contributions, operating purpose, and absence of commercial ownership interest)?

No → Not subject to the incremental industry-specific guidance

Yes ↓

Is the organization an all investor-owned entity or does it provide dividends, lower costs, or other economic benefits directly and proportionately to its owners, members, or participants, such as mutual insurance entities, credit unions, farm and rural electric cooperatives, and employee benefit plans.

Yes → Not subject to the incremental industry-specific guidance

No ↓

Does the organization meet the criteria to be considered a government?

Yes → Not subject to the incremental industry-specific guidance

No ↓

The organization is subject to the incremental industry-specific guidance included in the Not-for-Profit Entities Topic of the FASB ASC. It is important to note that additional incremental industry-specific guidance exists for not-for-profit, business-oriented health care entities (see FASB ASC 954).

Fund accounting

A commonly used tool

Many NFPs use fund accounting for internal recordkeeping purposes. Some include fund information in their external financial reports. Prior to the issuance of FASB No. 117, *Financial Statements of Not-for-Profit Organizations*, NFP organizations were required to report fund information in their external financial statements.

FASB ASC 958, *Not-for-Profit Entities,* changed the requirement to report information about funds. Instead, FASB ASC 958 focuses on reporting aggregated information about the entity as a whole. It requires reporting aggregated information about an organization's net assets that are classified based solely on donor-imposed restrictions. Organizations are allowed to present disaggregated information, such as fund information, as long as the information required by FASB ASC 958 is presented.

Knowledge check

4. Which is accurate of fund accounting?

    a. Some NFP organizations include fund information in their external financial reports.
    b. The financial statements presented by NFPs are based on fund accounting.
    c. NFP organizations may not use fund accounting for internal recordkeeping purposes.
    d. NFP organizations report one class of net assets.

Measuring performance

Many of the key performance measures for a business do not work for most NFP entities. For example, a key performance indicator for most business entities is the "bottom line" measurement of profit or loss. The bottom line indicates how effective an entity is in achieving its goal of generating profits for the owners. However, generating profits for the owners is not a goal for NFP entities.

These entities have no owners, often provide goods and services to constituents without a fee, and often seek resources from individuals and entities that do not expect economic benefits from the resources provided. Therefore, the "bottom line" is not the key performance indicator for NFP entities. There are several ways to evaluate how an entity is performing. NFP entities have significant flexibility in reporting results in their statement of activities, which can help a user understand the operations of such entities. Users can also utilize ratios and other tools to evaluate financial performance. Input, output, and outcome measures can be used to evaluate effectiveness and efficiency of an organization.

Reporting information in the statement of activities

The statement of activities reports revenues, gains, expenses, losses, and reclassifications for the period. The statement of activities focuses on the entity as a whole and must report certain totals for the period.

Entities have significant flexibility in displaying the required information in the statement of activities. The main requirement for this statement is that totals be reported for the amount of change in total net assets, net assets without donor restrictions, and net assets with donor restrictions.

One aspect of this flexibility is to report disaggregated information by using columns in the statement of activities. Entities may use several columns to present information as long as the required totals for the entity are reported.

Another aspect of this flexibility is how items are sequenced in the statement of activities. Revenues, gains, expenses, losses, and reclassifications can be arranged in a variety of orders. In addition, an entity may choose to report some intermediate measure of operations, such as operating revenues over expenses. If a measure of operations is reported, the term "operations" must be clear from the detail provided on the face of the statement or from a description contained in the notes to the financial statement.

The ability to report a measure of operations in the statement of activities allows an entity to provide important information about its financial performance for the period. It provides a means for an entity to "tell its story" about how it operated financially for the period. For example, an entity may consider some sources of revenues to be available to support operations and other sources of revenues to be invested to provide investment income long-term.

When a measure of operations is not used, revenues, gains and losses, and reclassifications are typically reported separate from expenses. The difference between the two categories is simply reported as change in net assets.

Consider the following examples of entities that may want to report certain items separately from the items included in a measure of operations:

1. Entity A depends on annual donations and grants for a major source of support each year. It also has a policy of not including bequests as part of operations, although these funds are without donor restrictions. The entity invests these funds and only spends the income. The entity reports all bequests separate from its measure of operations.
2. Entity B has a substantial amount of endowments. It follows a total return approach in managing these funds. Its policy is to only make available 5% of the fair value of the endowment to support operations each year. Any additional return from the investments is retained and invested. It reports only the 5% return in the measure of operations. The additional return is reported separate from its measure of operations.
3. Entity C charges for its services based on ability to pay. It wishes to report contributions separate from a measure of operations. The measure of operations provides important information about the

level of support needed to sustain the organization. The entity reports all contributions separate from its measure of operations.

To illustrate the preceding, consider the following information for Entities A, B, and C:

Contributions	$20,000
Bequest	$30,000
Fee revenue	$70,000
Investment income	$40,000 (for Entity B, assume the 5% limit equates to $25,000)
Total expenses	$145,000

A partial statement of activities for the three entities with a performance measure would appear as shown in exhibit 4-3.

Exhibit 4-3: Measure of operations

	Entity A	Entity B	Entity C
Operating revenues			
Contributions	$ 20,000	$ 50,000	$–
Fee revenue	70,000	70,000	70,000
Investment income	40,000	25,000	40,000
Total operating revenue	130,000	145,000	110,000
Operating expenses	145,000	145,000	145,000
Income (loss) from operations	(15,000)	–	(35,000)
Contributions	30,000	–	50,000
Investment income	–	15,000	–
Change in net assets	$ 15,000	$ 15,000	$ 15,000

Note that exhibit 4-3 is reflecting the different results from the use of different measures of operations between three entities in one exhibit. Had only one entity been presented, the financial statement line items and captions would have appeared differently (for example, Entity C would not have had a contributions line in the operating revenues section).

Ratios and other tools

Many stakeholders are interested in the financial performance of NFP entities. Resource providers (for example, individual donors, foundations, and creditors), boards of directors, and other oversight bodies are just some examples. However, financial statements contain a lot of numbers and can be difficult to analyze. Numbers by themselves contain little information. There is limited value to saying that items such as cash, net assets, or certain revenues or expenses are of some amount.

Comparing the financial statements among different NFP entities can have limited value because entities can vary greatly in size and scope, making direct dollar value comparisons difficult. However, as illustrated in the following, there are tools that can be used to bring more meaning to the numbers presented on financial statements.

Tools to bring more meaning to the numbers

The first tool is trend analysis. This technique tracks the change in financial statement accounts over a period of time and can be very useful in identifying significant changes. Both dollar and percentage changes can be used with trend analysis. This tool is very helpful in analyzing an organization's activities over a period of time.

A second tool that can be used is common size statements. The items in the statement of financial position can be stated as a percentage of total assets, and the items in the statement of activities can be stated in terms of either total revenues or total expenses. These percentages can reveal important information about an NFP organization's finances and also lend themselves to comparisons between different entities. For example, an entity can determine that 75% of its expenses are going toward program expenses. It can also compare this percentage to what other similar entities are spending.

Another tool that can be used to analyze financial information is ratio analysis. Ratios are often used to express relationships between two elements on the same financial statement or for two elements from different statements. In addition to providing information about the relationship between items in the financial statements, ratios are another good way to make comparisons between entities of different sizes. For example, an organization's net assets without donor restrictions can be expressed as a percentage of total operating expenses, giving information about the level of reserves without donor restrictions.

Exhibit 4-4 provides a list of some of the ratios an NFP entity may want to use.

Exhibit 4-4: Ratios for NFP entities

Type of ratio	Purpose	Ratio
Liquidity	Ability to pay current debt	Current assets/ Current liabilities
Operating strength	Ability to meet future expenses	Net assets without donor restrictions/ Operating expenses
Debt ratio	Reliance on debt to finance assets	Debt/ Total assets
Program effectiveness	Amount spent on meeting the organization's goals	Program expenses/ Total expenses
Fund-raising efficiency	Ability to raise funds in an economical manner	Fund-raising expense/ Public support

Several ratios for NFP entities are closely monitored by organizations such as the Better Business Bureau, American Institute of Philanthropy, and GuideStar. These organizations are often interested in ratios that reflect how much of an NFP's resources are going to program service and how efficient entities are in fund-raising activities. The websites of these organizations can be found at the following web addresses:

- Better Business Bureau — www.give.org
- American Institute of Philanthropy — www.charitywatch.org
- GuideStar — www.guidestar.org

Knowledge check

5. Which is accurate of using ratios and other tools?

    a. Many stakeholders are interested in the financial performance of NFP entities.
    b. There is limited value in saying that items such as cash, net assets, or certain revenues or expenses are of some amount.
    c. Financial statements contain a lot of numbers that make them easy to analyze.
    d. A tool that cannot be used is trend analysis.

6. Which is accurate of using ratios and other tools?

    a. Comparing the financial statements among different NFP entities can have limited value because entities can vary greatly in size and scope, making direct dollar value comparisons difficult.

    b. Common size statements are a tool that cannot be used.

    c. There are no tools that can be used to bring more meaning to the numbers presented on financial statements.

    d. There is no ratio that measures fund-raising efficiency.

Input, output, and outcomes

There are several ways to judge the performance of an NFP organization. The previous section describes evaluating the performance of an entity based on the amount of resources an entity spends on providing program services (the amount an entity spends to carry out its purpose) versus management and general expense and fund-raising activities. For most entities, a higher percentage of resources spent on program services is considered a positive performance indicator.

Although this type of measure is useful, it lacks the ability to indicate how effectively an entity uses it resources to meet its objectives. For example, an entity may spend 80% of its resources on providing a particular program service but may be ineffective in reaching the goals of that program. Just spending resources on providing a service is not an effective measure of performance.

FASB recognizes the limitations of traditional financial statements for assessing performance of NFP entities. In FASB Concepts Statement No. 4, the need for a different type of information to measure the performance of NFP entities is identified. The statement calls for reporting information about service efforts (how resources are used to provide different programs or services) in the financial statements.

The statement also discusses the idea that, ideally, information about service accomplishments should be provided as part of financial reporting. The statement recognizes the difficulties in measuring and reporting program accomplishments and the need for research to determine whether service effort and accomplishment measurements can be developed that meet the characteristics required to be included in the financial statements of NFP entities.

Four categories of service efforts and accomplishment measures	
	Input measures
	Output measures
	Outcome measures
	Efficiency measures

The measures in the preceding chart can provide information on the amount of effort expended to carry out a program (inputs), the level of services provided (outputs), what effect that service has had on the stated objectives of the program (outcomes), and comparison of the level of inputs with outputs or outcomes (efficiency).

Entities are very accustomed to reporting input measures. For example, financial resources dedicated to specific programs are reported in the financial statements. Many entities also report nonfinancial information about effort expended, such as hours expended to meet a program goal.

Output measures are often stated in nonfinancial terms. For example, a university may report the number of students that graduated, or a homeless shelter may report the number of people housed.

Outcome measures should gauge the level of accomplishment of a program goal. For example, a program designed to teach reading to adults may use the literacy rate for the area served as an outcome measure. These measures strive to assess the effectiveness of a program at meeting its goal. A limitation of outcome measures is that they can be affected by many factors other than a specific program. However, when used over a period of time, they can become a key performance measure of a program's effectiveness.

Often, the final step an entity can take in using service efforts and accomplishments is to measure efficiency. This process computes inputs, outputs, or outcome indicators and provides a measure of how efficient an entity is in achieving program goals.

So inputs, outputs, outcomes, and their relative ratios all can be used in assessing the performance of NFPs. Many foundations and other funding entities are requiring NFPs to report this type of information in their funding requests.

Knowledge check

7. Which is accurate of performance indicators?

    a. There are several ways to judge the performance of an NFP organization.
    b. Just spending resources on providing a service is an effective measure of performance.
    c. For most entities, a higher percentage of resources spent on program services is considered a negative performance indicator.
    d. FASB does not recognize the limitations of traditional financial statements for assessing performance of NFP entities.

8. Which is accurate of service efforts and accomplishment measures?

    a. Outcome measures are a category of service efforts and accomplishment measures.
    b. In FASB Concepts Statement No. 4, the need for a different type of information to measure the performance of NFP entities is not identified.
    c. Efficiency measures are not a category of service efforts and accomplishment measures.
    d. Input measures are used to report the level of services provided.

Tax-exempt organizations have annual reporting requirements with the IRS; those requirements are as follows:

- Form 990 is required for organizations with gross revenues greater than $200,000 and total assets greater than $500,000.
- Form 990-EZ can be filed instead of Form 990 if the entity has annual gross receipts of less than $200,000 and total assets at the end of the year less than $500,000.
- Organizations with annual gross receipts of less than $50,000 may submit Form 990-N instead of Form 990 or 990EZ.

It is important that all exempt organizations stay apprised of the information provided at https://www.irs.gov/charities-non-profits/. Most states also have their own registration and filing requirements, some of which include audited financial statements.

Another source of regulation that NFPs often encounter is the requirement for audits performed under *Government Auditing Standards* (the Yellow Book) and the Uniform Guidance. These are most commonly required due to the receipt of federal funding or by law. Numerous publications and CPE courses have been written about this topic.

Summary

NFP organizations have different environmental factors than do business organizations. They receive contributions, have an operating purpose other than making a profit, and typically have no owners. Because of these differences, NFP organizations have different reporting objectives.

NFPs have several ways to report and evaluate how they are performing. Organizations have significant flexibility in reporting results in their statement of activities, which can help a user understand the operations of such organizations. Users can also utilize ratios and other tools to evaluate financial performance. Input, output, and outcome measures can be used to evaluate effectiveness and efficiency of an organization.

Practice questions

1. Which is a characteristic that distinguishes NFP organizations from business enterprises?

    a. Contributions (nonreciprocal transactions).
    b. Operating purposes other than to provide goods or services at a profit.
    c. Absence of ownership interests like those of business enterprises.
    d. All of the above.

2. Which is **not** a financial reporting objective of NFP organizations?

    a. Determining profitability.
    b. Making rational decisions about the allocation of resources.
    c. Assessing the services that the entity provides and its ability to continue to provide those services.
    d. Assessing how managers have discharged their stewardship responsibilities.

3. Which is a class of net assets for NFP organizations under Accounting Standards Update (ASU) No. 2016-14?

    a. Unrestricted net assets.
    b. Net investment in capital assets.
    c. Temporarily restricted net assets.
    d. Net Assets without donor restrictions.

4. Which is a unique accounting and reporting practice of NFP organizations?

    a. Contributions (nonreciprocal transactions).
    b. Required financial statements.
    c. Net assets.
    d. All of the above.

5. Which characteristic used to determine if an entity is a government can be rebutted based on compelling, relevant evidence?

    a. The majority of governing board members are appointed by government entities.
    b. The entity has the power to enact and enforce a tax levy.
    c. The entity has the ability to directly issue federally tax-exempt debt.
    d. A government is able to unilaterally dissolve the entity, with the entity's net assets reverting to a government.

6. Which ratio would be the most useful in determining an organization's ability to meet future expenses?

    a. Liquidity.
    b. Debt ratio.
    c. Operating strength.
    d. Program effectiveness.

7. The amount of dollars spent on housing the homeless is what type of measure?

    a. Input.
    b. Output.
    c. Outcome.
    d. Efficiency.

8. The number of people sleeping in the homeless shelter is what type of measure?

    a. Input.
    b. Output.
    c. Outcome.
    d. Efficiency.

Case study: Feed the Hungry of Radford

Case study: Background information

Feed the Hungry of Radford (FHR) is a local NFP entity governed by people who volunteer to serve on the board of directors. FHR focuses on providing meals to homeless people in the community. The organization receives its annual operating funds from donations made by individuals and businesses in the community.

The following is condensed financial information from the last year:

Statement of financial position information

Current assets	$25,000	Current liabilities	$10,000
Noncurrent assets	$50,000	Noncurrent liabilities	$5,000
		Total liabilities	$15,000
Total assets	$75,000	Net assets without donor restrictions	$60,000

Case study: Feed the Hungry of Radford (continued)

Statement of activities information

Contributions	$100,000
Other revenues	10,000
Total revenues	110,000
Program expense	$70,000
Management and general expense	20,000
Fund-raising expenses	10,000
Total expense	100,000
Change in net assets without donor restrictions	$10,000

Case study exercise 1

From the preceding financial information, compute the following ratios. Use the right column to record your answers.

Ratio	Answer
Liquidity	
Operating strength	
Debt ratio	
Program effectiveness	
Fund-raising efficiency	

Case study: Feed the Hungry of Radford (continued)

Case study exercise 2

How should the following service efforts and accomplishments be classified for FHR (input, output, outcome, or efficiency measure)? Use the right column to record your answers.

Items	Answer
Cost per meal served	
Number of meals served	
Hours spent preparing the meals	
Number of malnutrition cases reported	
Amount spent on food	
Number of people served	

Appendix A

EXCERPT OF APPENDIX A OF CHAPTER 5 OF AICPA AUDIT AND ACCOUNTING GUIDE *NOT-FOR-PROFIT ENTITIES*[1]

---

[1] From Audit and Accounting Guide *Not-for-Profit Entities*. ©2019, AICPA. All rights reserved. This product is available at www.aicpastore.com.

Appendix A—Excerpt From AICPA Financial Reporting White Paper *Measurement of Fair Value for Certain Transactions of Not-for-Profit Entities.*[2]

A-1 Not-for-profit entities face various challenges in applying the provisions of Financial Accounting Standards Board *Accounting Standards Codification* 820, *Fair Value Measurement*, in part because markets do not exist for certain assets and liabilities. To assist practitioners, on October 14, 2011, the AICPA issued the white paper Measurement of Fair Value for Certain Transactions of Not-for-Profit Entities. The following excerpt provides assistance for measuring unconditional promises to give cash or other financial assets due in one year or more.

Unconditional Promises to Give Cash

1. Financial Accounting Standards Board (FASB) *Accounting Standards Codification* (ASC) 958-605,[3] in discussing measurement principles for contributions, generally requires not-for-profit entities (NFPs) to measure at fair value recognized contributions of cash or other assets (for example, marketable securities, land, buildings, use of facilities or utilities, materials and supplies, other goods or services) and unconditional promises to give those items in the future.

2. The discussion of fair value measurements in FASB ASC 820-10-35 includes an exit price approach (that is, the price that would be received for a promise to give [asset] in an exchange involving hypothetical market participants, determined under current market conditions). Because no market exists for unconditional promises to give, assumptions about what a hypothetical acquirer would pay for these assets (the right to receive from the donor the cash flow inherent in the promise) are necessary in determining fair value. FASB ASC 820-10-35 and its interpretive guidance in FASB ASC 820-10-55 emphasize that because fair value is a market-based (not an entity-specific) measurement, the exit price is determined without regard to whether an entity intends to sell or hold an asset or a liability that is measured at fair value.

3. Paragraphs 4–32 address the application of FASB ASC 820-10-35 in determining the fair value of a promise to give cash at a date one year or more in the future. This white paper does not discuss the fair value of a promise to give nonfinancial assets. It also does not discuss how to determine the fair value of unconditional promises to give that are due in less than one year. As explained in FASB ASC 958-605-30-6, unconditional promises to give that are expected to be

---

[2] As a benefit of AICPA membership, all AICPA members can access the AICPA White Paper *Measurement of Fair Value for Certain Transactions of Not-for-Profit Entities* at www.aicpa.org/InterestAreas/FRC/IndustryInsights/Pages/FV_and_Disclosures_NFP.aspx.

[3] Pursuant to Financial Accounting Standards Board (FASB) Statement No. 168, *The* FASB Accounting Standards Codification *and the Hierarchy of Generally Accepted Accounting Principles—a replacement of FASB Statement No. 162, FASB Accounting Standards Codification* (ASC) is the sole source of authoritative generally accepted accounting principles. To aid readers in using this white paper, as a drafting convention in referencing FASB ASC, this white paper sometimes references pronouncements that were issued prior to the effective date of FASB ASC and from which the FASB ASC paragraphs are derived.

---

collected in less than one year may be measured at net realizable value because that amount results in a reasonable estimate of fair value.

What Is the Unit of Account for an Unconditional Promise to Give That Is Expected to Be Collected in One Year or More?

4.   For an unconditional promise to give that is expected to be collected in one year or more, the unit of account implied in FASB ASC 958-605 is the individual (stand-alone) promise to give.[4] That means that the focus of the fair value measurement is on the individual (stand-alone) promise to give in which the exit price represents the amount that a hypothetical market participant would pay to acquire the right to receive from the donor the cash flows inherent in the promise to pay the NFP. The Financial Reporting Executive Committee (FinREC) believes that, consistent with the guidance in FASB ASC 820-10-35-17 on the measurement of the fair value of liabilities, it is appropriate to assume when measuring the fair value of a promise to give that the cash flows received by the hypothetical acquirer would be the same as the cash flows that would be received by the NFP and that no additional credit risk needs to be considered as a result of a hypothetical change in ownership.

What Valuation Technique(s) Should an NFP Use to Measure the Fair Value of an Unconditional Promise to Give That Is Expected to Be Collected in One Year or More?

5.   FASB ASC 820-10-35-24A provides that valuation techniques consistent with the market approach, income approach, cost approach, or all three should be used to measure fair value. Paragraphs 3A–3G of FASB ASC 820-10-55 explain those valuation techniques.

6.   FASB ASC 820-10-35-24 clarifies that "[a] reporting entity shall use valuation techniques that are appropriate in the circumstances and for which sufficient data are available to measure fair value, maximizing the use of relevant observable inputs and minimizing the use of unobservable inputs." For an unconditional promise to give that is expected to be collected in one year or more, FinREC believes that a present value (PV) technique (an application of the income approach) will be the most prevalent valuation technique used to measure fair value. In reaching that conclusion, FinREC observes that the market approach typically would not be operational for measuring the fair value of unconditional promises to give cash because no market exists, and the cost approach is not used for valuing financial assets, such as promises to give.

---

[4] In practice, some not-for-profit entities (NFPs) have pooled unconditional promises to give with certain similar characteristics. The Financial Reporting Executive Committee (FinREC) believes that such pooling is permissible in circumstances in which the measurement of fair value would not be materially different from a measurement that considers each unconditional promise to give as the unit of account.

PV Techniques

7. Paragraphs 4–20 of FASB ASC 820-10-55 discuss PV techniques. FASB ASC 820-10-55-5 states that

> [p]resent value (that is, an application of the income approach) is a tool used to link future amounts (for example, cash flows or values) to a present amount using a discount rate. A fair value measurement of an asset or a liability using a present value technique captures all of the following elements from the perspective of market participants at the measurement date:
>
> a. An estimate of future cash flows for the asset or liability being measured.
> b. Expectations about possible variations in the amount and timing of the cash flows representing the uncertainty inherent in the cash flows.
> c. The time value of money, represented by the rate on risk-free monetary assets that have maturity dates or durations that coincide with the period covered by the cash flows and pose neither uncertainty in timing nor risk of default to the holder (that is, a risk-free interest rate). For present value computations denominated in nominal U.S. dollars, the yield curve for U.S. Treasury securities determines the appropriate risk-free interest rate.
> d. The price for bearing the uncertainty inherent in the cash flows (that is, a risk premium).
> e. Other factors that market participants would take into account in the circumstances.
> f. For a liability, the nonperformance risk relating to that liability, including the reporting entity's (that is, the obligor's) own credit risk.

8. Risk and uncertainty associated with the amount, timing, or both, of cash flows of an asset (or a liability) are key considerations when measuring fair value because risk-averse market participants would demand compensation for bearing the uncertainty inherent in the cash flows (the risk premium).[5] Paragraphs 7–8 of FASB ASC 820-10-55 explain that

> [a] fair value measurement using present value techniques is made under conditions of uncertainty because the cash flows used are estimates rather than known amounts. In many cases, both the amount and timing of the cash flows are uncertain. Even contractually fixed amounts, such as the payments on a loan, are uncertain if there is risk of default.
>
> Market participants generally seek compensation (that is, a risk premium) for bearing the uncertainty inherent in the cash flows of an asset or a liability. A fair value measurement should include a risk premium reflecting the amount that market participants would demand as compensation for the uncertainty inherent in the cash flows. Otherwise, the measurement would not faithfully represent fair value. In some cases, determining the appropriate risk

---

[5] The FASB ASC glossary term *promise to give* notes that "the recipient of a promise to give has a right to expect that the promised assets will be transferred in the future, and the maker has a social and moral obligation, and generally a legal obligation, to make the promised transfer." As noted in paragraph 108 of FASB Statement No. 116, *Accounting for Contributions Received and Contributions Made*, in developing FASB Statement No. 116, FASB found that although legal remedies are available, they are seldom necessary because promises generally are kept. FinREC believes, however, that in many (if not most) cases, uncertainty will exist; therefore, it will be necessary to consider risk in a fair value measurement.

---

premium might be difficult. However, the degree of difficulty alone is not a sufficient reason to exclude a risk premium.

9. FinREC observes that the requisite risk assessment requires judgments and that those judgments are significant in some cases. In making that assessment, consistent with FASB ASC 820-10-35-54A, FinREC believes that an NFP need not undertake exhaustive efforts to obtain information from or about the donor. Rather, the NFP would assess the risk associated with the promise to give using information that is reasonably available in the circumstances, considering factors specific to the donor and promise to give. FinREC believes that those factors may include, but are not limited to, the following:

- The ability of the donor to pay (credit risk), which may be indicated by published credit ratings (for example, a credit rating might be available for an enterprise that is a donor or comparable to the donor); financial analysis (for example, cash flow and ratio analysis); or credit reports for an individual donor
- Factors specific to the donor that might be relevant in assessing the donor's commitment to honor its promise, such as the extent to which the donor is committed to, or otherwise involved in, the activities of the NFP (for example, whether the donor is a member of the governing board); the donor's history of charitable giving and involvement with charitable organizations, including, but not limited to, the NFP; and the donor's financial circumstances and history (past bankruptcies or defaults); financial condition (including other debt); current employment (including its stability); earnings potential over the term of the promise; and personal circumstances (including family situation, age, and health)
- Risk factors that affect certain groups of donors (for example, economic conditions in certain geographical areas or industry sectors)
- The NFP's prior experience in collecting similar types of promises to give, including the extent to which the NFP has enforced the promises
- Whether the underlying asset is held in an irrevocable trust or escrow, which may reduce default risk

10. FASB ASC 820-10-55 discusses two PV techniques: (*a*) the traditional or discount rate adjustment (DRA) technique and (*b*) the expected PV (EPV) technique, which may be applied using one of two methods. Those PV techniques differ in how they adjust for risk. Key differences are summarized in the following table:

	DRA	*EPV Method 1*	*EPV Method 2*
Cash Flows	Single set of cash flows (contractual or promised, most likely).[6]	Expected (probability-weighted) cash flows (or expected value), adjusted for general market (systematic) risk by subtracting the cash risk premium. The risk-adjusted expected cash flows represent a certainty-equivalent cash flow.	Expected (probability-weighted) cash flows (or expected value).
	The single set of cash flows are conditional cash flows (in other words, contractual or promised cash flows are conditional on the event of no default by the debtor).	The risk-adjusted expected cash flows are not conditional upon the occurrence of specific events because they are probability weighted.	The expected cash flows are not conditional upon the occurrence of specific events because they are probability weighted.

---

[6] Such nonprobability-weighted cash flows are referred to in this white paper as projected cash flows to distinguish them from expected cash flows, which are probability weighted.

	DRA	EPV Method 1	EPV Method 2
Discount Rate	Risk-adjusted discount rate derived from observed rates of return for comparable assets or liabilities that are traded in the market (that is, a market rate of return that corresponds to an observed market rate associated with such conditional cash flows and that, therefore, represents the amount that market participants would demand for bearing the uncertainty inherent in such cash flows).	Risk-free interest rate (for example, yield to maturity on U.S. Treasuries).	Risk-free interest rate (for example, yield to maturity on U.S. Treasuries), adjusted for general market (systematic) risk by adding risk premium. The risk-adjusted discount rate represents the expected rate of return that corresponds to an expected rate associated with such probability-weighted cash flows.

What Are Some of the Key Issues That an NFP Should Consider in Determining Which PV Technique to Use to Measure the Fair Value of an Unconditional Promise to Give That Is Expected to Be Collected in One Year or More?

11. Conceptually, the three PV methods discussed in the chart in the previous paragraph should give the same results. FinREC observes that in practice, however, certain techniques may be easier, more practical, or more appropriate to apply to certain facts and circumstances. FASB ASC 820-10-55-4 states that the "present value technique used to measure fair value will depend on facts and circumstances specific to the asset or liability being measured (for example, whether prices for comparable assets or liabilities can be observed in the market) and the availability of sufficient data."

12. A DRA technique using promised cash flows and observable market rates that reflect expectations about future defaults may be easier to apply at initial recognition than the EPV techniques, which require an NFP to probability weight the cash flows or estimate the systematic risk premium. However, to account for the unconditional promises to give in subsequent periods, the NFP must be able to identify when the level of defaults on its promises surpasses the level incorporated in the discount rate that it used for initial recognition, so that it can recognize an allowance for uncollectible promises on a timely basis if the actual uncollectible amounts exceed the amounts originally projected. This can be particularly challenging if the discount rate used is a market rate for which the level of default incorporated in the rate is not publicly available. The use of most likely cash flows, rather than promised cash flows, and a discount rate that is consistent with those cash flows will mitigate some of the challenges for subsequent measurement. That DRA technique is discussed in the next paragraph.

13. Although it might appear that the DRA technique may be easy to apply because it does not require an NFP to probability weight the cash flows or estimate the systematic risk premium, as required by the EPV technique, FinREC observes that the DRA technique using promised cash flows may be impractical to apply. FinREC observes that if an NFP uses the DRA technique with promised cash flows, it must use a discount rate that reflects expectations about future defaults, and the NFP must be able to identify when the level of defaults on its unconditional promises to give surpasses the level incorporated in the discount rate it used. This is particularly challenging if the discount rate used is a market rate, such as for unsecured borrowings in which the level of default incorporated in the rate is typically not available. If the NFP does not identify the level of defaults incorporated in the discount rate, it would be unable to timely report a credit impairment loss when the actual uncollectible amounts exceed the amounts originally projected. Thus, the benefit of avoiding the calculation of probability-weighted cash flows on initial measurement (if using the DRA technique with promised cash flows) would be substantially negated by the fact that the NFP would nevertheless have to estimate the cash flows initially expected when determining the allowance for doubtful accounts in subsequent measurements.[7]

14. A DRA technique that uses most likely cash flows (rather than promised cash flows) might be practical to apply because the cash flows initially projected are known, but that technique requires the NFP to use a discount rate that reflects market participant assumptions that are consistent with risks inherent in most likely cash flows to avoid double counting or omitting the effects of risk factors. As explained in paragraph 19, the discount rate would be higher than the risk-free rate used in EPV method 1 or the discount rate used in EPV method 2 because most likely cash flows are uncertain, but the discount rate would be lower than the discount rate used with promised cash flows because some of the uncertainty of promised cash flows is removed in the determination of most likely cash flows. Because the three PV techniques trade off the ease of determining a discount rate against the ease of determining the cash flows, FinREC observes that no one PV technique is inherently better than another for measuring unconditional promises to give.

15. FinREC observes that in estimating fair value, an entity is not precluded from using fair value estimates provided by third parties, such as valuation specialists, in circumstances in which a reporting entity has determined that the estimates provided by those parties are determined in accordance with FASB ASC 820-10-35. For example, in using a PV technique, valuation specialists may be helpful in determining a discount rate that is consistent with the cash flows used.

---

[7] The discussion in paragraphs 12–14 assumes that the NFP does not elect to report contributions receivable pursuant to an election under FASB ASC 825, *Financial Instruments*. Instead, the discussion assumes that an NFP initially measures contributions receivable at fair value using present value techniques, which then is used as cost. In subsequent periods, that cost is amortized, with the interest element reported as additional contribution revenue, and a valuation allowance is reported to reflect credit impairment occurring after initial measurement.

What Are the Key Pricing Inputs When Using a PV Technique?

16. Key pricing inputs should reflect the factors that market participants would consider in setting a price for the promise to give. The FASB ASC 820-10-35 fair value hierarchy prioritizes market observable inputs but also allows for the use of unobservable (internally derived) inputs when relevant market observable inputs are unavailable. When using a PV technique, two key pricing inputs are the cash flows and discount rate. The factors considered in determining the cash flows and discount rate used should be documented.

17. As noted in FASB ASC 820-10-55-6(c), to avoid double counting or omitting the effects of risk factors, discount rates should reflect assumptions that are consistent with those inherent in the cash flows. For example, a discount rate that reflects the uncertainty in expectations about future defaults is appropriate if using contractual cash flows of a loan. That same rate should not be used if using expected (that is, probability-weighted) cash flows because the expected cash flows already reflect assumptions about the uncertainty of future defaults.

18. The cash flows used in a PV technique differ depending on the method used. Following is an illustration of cash flow estimates under the three methods (DRA, EPV method 1, and EPV method 2). Assume that an NFP holds a promise to give $100 in one year. The NFP believes that there is a 70 percent chance that it will collect the full amount, a 20 percent chance that it will collect $80, and a 10 percent chance that it will collect nothing. Under EPV method 2, expected cash flow would be calculated as follows:

$100 x 70% =	$70
$80 x 20% =	$16
$0 x 10% =	$0
	$86

Under EPV method 1, the expected cash flow would be less than $86 because it would be adjusted (reduced) for systematic risk. Because of the challenges in determining an adjustment for systematic risk, utilization of EPV method 1 may not be practical. Under the DRA technique, both the promised cash flow and most likely cash flow are $100.

19. FASB ASC 820-10-55-6 discusses general principles for determining the discount rate when applying PV techniques. FinREC believes that the discount rate used would fall on a continuum between the risk-free rate (minimum) and unsecured borrowing rate (maximum).

Risk-free rate   Unsecured borrowing rate

Where the rate falls on the continuum would depend on the extent to which risk factors such as those discussed in paragraph 9 have been incorporated into the projected cash flows. (The lowest discount rate would be used for EPV method 1, and the highest discount rate would be used for the DRA technique using contractual cash flows,[8] as discussed in paragraphs 21–32.) The relationship between cash flows and discount rates is depicted as follows:

This diagram depicts the inverse relationship between risks being incorporated in projected cash flows and risks being incorporated in discount rates (that is, the discount rate increases as projected cash flows incorporate fewer risk factors and vice versa).

EPV Method 1

20. When using EPV method 1, the risk-adjusted expected cash flows are discounted by the risk-free interest rate, which may be indicated by the yield to maturity on U.S. Treasuries. The risk-free interest rate is appropriate in this case because all risk is built into the expected cash flows, which therefore represent a certainty-equivalent cash flow. As discussed in FASB ASC 820-10-55-15, EPV method 1 adjusts the expected cash flows for the systematic (market) risk by subtracting a cash risk premium in arriving at risk-adjusted expected cash flows. However, as previously discussed, determining a certainty-equivalent cash flow typically would be impracticable for unconditional promises to give.

EPV Method 2

21. When using EPV method 2, the expected cash flows are discounted by a risk-adjusted rate, which is determined based on the risk-free interest rate, adjusted for general market (systematic) risk by adding a risk premium.

22. In EPV method 2, some but not all risk is built into the expected cash flows. The expected cash flows are probability weighted and, therefore, adjusted for the likelihood of possible outcomes affecting the timing and amount of the cash flows. Probability weighting is not enough, however. It is also necessary to adjust for the risk premium that market participants would seek for accepting uncertainty. The following example illustrates this point:

> Asset B is a *certain* undiscounted cash flow of $10,000 due 10 years hence (a U.S. Treasury instrument is an example of asset B). Asset E has an *expected* undiscounted cash flow of $10,000 due 10 years hence; however, the actual cash flow from asset E may be as high as $12,000 or as low as $8,000 or some other amount within that range. A risk-averse individual

---

[8] For an unconditional promise to give, the contractual cash flows are the amounts promised by the donor, which are referred to as promised cash flows in this white paper.

would pay something less for asset E than asset B because of the uncertainty involved. Although the expected cash flow of $10,000 incorporates the uncertainty in cash flows from asset E, that amount does not incorporate the premium that market participants demand for bearing that uncertainty.

23. In EPV method 2, the compensation that market participants would seek for accepting uncertainty (the risk premium) is built into the discount rate. The risk-adjusted discount rate represents an expected rate of return that corresponds to an expected rate associated with such probability-weighted cash flows.

DRA

24. When using the DRA technique, the projected cash flows are discounted by a risk-adjusted rate. As discussed in FASB ASC 820-10-55-10

> the [DRA] technique uses a single set of cash flows from the range of possible estimated amounts, whether contractual or promised (as is the case for a bond) or most likely cash flows. In all cases, those cash flows are conditional upon the occurrence of specified events (for example, contractual or promised cash flows for a bond are conditional on the event of no default by the debtor).

25. The risk-adjusted discount rate used in the DRA technique is derived from observed rates of return for comparable assets or liabilities that are traded in the market. Accordingly, the contractual, promised, or most likely cash flows are discounted at an observed or estimated market rate for such conditional cash flows (that is, a market rate of return). Therefore, it represents the amount that market participants would demand for bearing the uncertainty inherent in such cash flows. In circumstances in which the projected cash flows already reflect assumptions about future defaults, NFPs should apply a discount rate that is commensurate with the reduced risk inherent in the cash flows that anticipate defaults, in order to avoid double counting that credit risk, as discussed in FASB ASC 820-10-55-6.

26. Determining the observed rate of return for comparable assets that are traded in the market requires an analysis of market data for comparable assets. FASB ASC 820-10-55-11 explains that "[c]omparability is established by considering the nature of the cash flows (for example, whether the cash flows are contractual or noncontractual and are likely to respond similarly to changes in economic conditions), as well as other factors (for example, credit standing, collateral, duration, restrictive covenants, and liquidity)." As a basis for assessing comparability, FinREC believes that best practice is for the NFP to assess the likelihood that the donor will not honor its promise to give (default risk), as well as the risk premium reflecting the amount that market participants would demand because of the risk (uncertainty) in the cash flows.[9]

---

[9] FinREC believes that a promise to give is different from a trade receivable. A promise to give arises from a donative intent. It is not an exchange transaction in which each of the parties to the exchange receives equivalent value and, generally, will be expected to exercise rights created by the exchange to enforce the terms of the

27. Market comparable data that might be relevant in determining the risk-adjusted discount rate used in the DRA technique will differ depending on the donor (for example, whether the donor is an individual, a corporation, or a foundation). Some examples follow.

28. If the donor is an individual, FinREC believes that the risk-adjusted discount rate might be determined using unsecured consumer lending rates that are generally available from published sources (major financial institutions). FinREC believes that best practice is to use those unsecured consumer lending rates in circumstances in which the credit characteristics of the donor are similar to the credit characteristics of those with unsecured debt.

29. FinREC believes that in applying the DRA technique using promised cash flows for promises from individuals, an unsecured consumer lending rate might be a starting point for determining an observable market interest rate. The NFP, however, may need to make adjustments to that rate, as discussed in paragraph 32, including, but not limited to, adjustments based on differences in the credit characteristics of the donor compared with the credit characteristics of borrowers of unsecured debt. (FinREC believes that such adjustments might be made based on the average credit characteristics of a homogeneous group of donors in circumstances in which the results would not be materially different from making such adjustments based on the specific credit characteristics of an individual donor.)

30. If the donor is a corporation, and the DRA technique using promised cash flows is used, FinREC believes that the risk-adjusted discount rate might be determined using the yield on publicly traded debt, whether issued by the corporation itself or a comparable corporation. FinREC believes that best practice is to use that yield on publicly traded debt in circumstances in which the promise to give is similar to the publicly traded debt. If the donor is a private foundation, FinREC believes that the risk-adjusted discount rate might be similarly determined using the yield on publicly traded debt, whether issued by the foundation itself, a comparable foundation, or a comparable corporation.[10]

---

transaction. FinREC believes that information derived from a trade receivable might be relevant in determining the discount rate used in the discount rate adjustment technique. However, adjustments to that information might be needed to incorporate the risk inherent in the cash flows in situations in which the NFP does not have a practice of enforcing its rights to receive promises to pay.

[10] In considering the yield on debt issued by a foundation or other NFP, FinREC believes that the relevant input is the taxable yield, not the tax-exempt yield.

---

31. In either case (whether the donor is a corporation or foundation), the NFP would consider factors specific to the promise, including its terms and risk, in assessing the extent to which the promise to give is similar to publicly traded debt. For example, FinREC believes that a promise to give a single fixed contribution at a future date likely would be more analogous to publicly traded zero coupon debt that pays a single amount at a future date than to a debt instrument that periodically pays interest or principal, or both.[11]

32. In all cases, the NFP would evaluate comparability and adjust available market data for differences, so that the risk-adjusted discount rate used to measure fair value (such as unsecured lending rates or yield on publicly traded debt) is reasonable when considered in the context of the donor and cash flows used. For example, as discussed in paragraphs 12–14, if the NFP uses most likely cash flows, rather than promised cash flows, to mitigate some of the challenges for subsequent measurement, an observed market rate based on promised cash flows (such as an unsecured lending rate or a yield on publicly traded debt) would be adjusted downward to reflect the fact that most likely cash flows incorporate an assessment of default.

---

[11] For publicly traded zero coupon debt, comparability should be established based on its remaining term to maturity. For a debt instrument that periodically pays interest, principal, or both, FinREC believes that comparability should be established based on its duration, not its remaining term to maturity. Duration refers to the weighted average term over which the debt cash flows will be received.

Exempt Organizations Glossary

Governmental terminology

Accounting system – The methods and records established to identify, assemble, analyze, classify, record, and report a government's transactions and to maintain accountability for the related assets and liabilities.

Accrual basis of accounting – The recording of financial effects on a government of transactions and other events and circumstances that have consequences for the government in the periods in which those transactions, events, and circumstances occur, rather than only in the periods in which cash is received or paid by the government.

Ad valorem tax – A tax based on value (such as a property tax).

Advance from other funds – An asset account used to record noncurrent portions of a long-term debt owed by one fund to another fund within the same reporting entity. (See **Due to other funds** and **interfund receivable/payable**).

Agency funds – A fund normally used to account for assets held by a government as an agent for individuals; private organizations; or other governments or other funds, or both.

Appropriation – A legal authorization granted by a legislative body to make expenditures and to incur obligations for specific purposes. An appropriation is usually limited in the amount and time it may be expended.

Assigned fund balance – A portion of fund balance that includes amounts that are constrained by the government's intent to be used for specific purposes, but that are neither restricted nor committed.

Basis of accounting – A term used to refer to *when* revenues, expenditures, expenses, and transfers, and related assets and liabilities are recognized in the accounts and reported in the financial statements. Specifically, it relates to the timing of the measurements made, regardless of the nature of the measurement. (See **Accrual basis of accounting, cash basis of accounting, and modified accrual basis of accounting**).

Bond – A written promise to pay a specified sum of money (the face value or principal amount) at a specified date or dates in the future (the maturity dates[s]), together with periodic interest at a specified rate. Sometimes, however, all or a substantial part of the interest is included in the face value of the security. The difference between a note and bond is that the latter is issued for a longer period and requires greater legal formality.

Business type activities – Those activities of a government carried out primarily to provide specific services in exchange for a specific user charge.

Capital grants – Grants restricted by the grantor for the acquisition or construction, or both, of (a) capital asset(s).

Capital projects fund – A fund used to account for and report financial resources that are restricted, committed, or assigned to expenditures for capital outlays, including the acquisition or construction of capital facilities and other capital assets. Capital project funds exclude those types of capital-related outflows financed by proprietary funds or for assets that will be held in trust for individuals, private organizations, or other governments.

Cash basis of accounting – A basis of accounting that requires the recognition of transactions only when cash is received or disbursed.

Committed fund balance – A portion of fund balance that includes amounts that can only be used for specific purposes pursuant to constraints imposed by formal action of the government's highest level of decision-making authority.

Consumption method – The method of accounting that requires the recognition of an expenditure or expense as inventories are used.

Contributed capital – Contributed capital is created when a general capital asset is *transferred* to a proprietary fund or when a grant is received that is externally restricted to capital acquisition or construction. Contributions restricted to capital acquisition and construction and capital assets received from developers are reported in the operating statement as a separate item after nonoperating revenues and expenses.

Debt service fund – A fund used to account for and report financial resources that are restricted, committed, or assigned to expenditure for principal and interest. Debt service funds should be used to report resources if legally mandated. Financial resources that are being accumulated for principal and interest maturing in future years should also be reported as debt service funds.

Deferred inflow of resources – An acquisition of net assets by a government that is applicable to a future reporting period.

Deferred outflow of resources – A consumption of net asset by a government that is applicable to a future reporting period.

Deficit – (a) The excess of the liabilities of a fund over its assets. (b) The excess of expenditures over revenues during an accounting period or, in the case of proprietary funds, the excess of expenses over revenues during an accounting period.

Disbursement – A payment made in cash or by check. Expenses are only recognized at the time physical cash is disbursed.

Due from other funds – A current asset account used to indicate an account reflecting amounts owed to a particular fund by another fund for goods sold or services rendered. This account includes only short-term obligations on an open account, not interfund loans.

Due to other funds – A current liability account reflecting amounts owed by a particular fund to another fund for goods sold or services rendered. This account includes only short-term obligations on an open account, not interfund loans.

Fund financial statements – Each fund has its own set of self-balancing accounts and fund financial statements that focus on information about the government's governmental, proprietary, and fiduciary fund types.

Enabling legislation – Legislation that authorizes a government to assess, levy, charge, or otherwise mandate payment of resources from external resource providers and includes a legally enforceable requirement that those resources be used for the specific purposes stipulated in the legislation.

Encumbrances – Commitments related to unperformed (executory) contracts for goods or services. Used in budgeting, encumbrances are *not* generally accepted accounting principles (GAAP) expenditures or liabilities but represent the estimated amount of expenditures that will ultimately result if unperformed contracts in process are completed.

Enterprise fund – A fund established to account for operations financed and operated in a manner similar to private business enterprises (such as gas, utilities, transit systems, and parking garages). Usually, the governing body intends that costs of providing goods or services to the general public be recovered primarily through user charges.

Expenditures – Decreases in net financial resources. Expenditures include current operating expenses requiring the present or future use of net current assets, debt service and capital outlays, intergovernmental grants, entitlements, and shared revenues.

Expenses – Outflows or other consumption of assets or incurrences of liabilities, or a combination of both, from delivering or producing goods, rendering services, or carrying out other activities that constitute the entity's ongoing major or central operations.

Fund – A fiscal and accounting entity with a self-balancing set of accounts in which cash and other financial resources, all related liabilities and residual equities, or balances, and changes therein, are recorded and segregated to carry on specific activities or attain certain objectives in accordance with special regulations, restrictions, or limitations.

Fund balance – The difference between fund assets and fund liabilities of the generic fund types within the governmental category of funds.

Fund type – The 11 generic funds that all transactions of a government are recorded into. The 11 fund types are as follows: general, special revenue, debt service, capital projects, permanent, enterprise, internal service, private purpose trust, pension trust, investment trust, and agency.

GASB – The Governmental Accounting Standards Board (GASB) was organized in 1984 by the Financial Accounting Foundation (FAF) to establish standards of financial accounting and reporting for state and local governmental entities. Its standards guide the preparation of external financial reports of those entities.

General fund – The fund within the governmental category used to account for all financial resources, except those required to be accounted for in another governmental fund.

General-purpose governments – Governmental entities that provide a range of services, such as states, cities, counties, towns, and villages.

Governmental funds – Funds used to account for the acquisition, use, and balances of spendable financial resources and the related current liabilities, except those accounted for in proprietary funds and fiduciary funds. Essentially, these funds are accounting segregations of financial resources. Spendable assets are assigned to a particular government fund type according to the purposes for which they may or must be used. Current liabilities are assigned to the fund type from which they are to be paid. The difference between the assets and liabilities of governmental fund types is referred to as *fund balance*. The measurement focus in these fund types is on the determination of financial position and changes in financial position (sources, uses, and balances of financial resources), rather than on net income determination.

Government-wide financial statements – Highly aggregated financial statements that present financial information for all assets (including infrastructure capital assets), liabilities, and net assets of a primary government and its component units, except for fiduciary funds. The government-wide financial statements use the economic resources measurement focus and accrual basis of accounting.

Infrastructure assets – Long-lived capital assets that normally are stationary in nature and can be preserved for a significantly greater number of years than most capital assets. Examples of infrastructure assets are roads, bridges, tunnels, drainage systems, water and sewer systems, dams, and lighting systems. Buildings, except those that are an ancillary part of a network of infrastructure assets, are not considered infrastructure assets.

Interfund receivable/payable – Activity between funds of a government reflecting amounts provided with a requirement for repayment, or sales and purchases of goods and services between funds approximating their external exchange value (also referred to as **interfund loans** or **interfund services provided and used**.

Internal service fund – A generic fund type within the proprietary category used to account for the financing of goods or services provided by one department or agency to other departments or agencies of a government, or to other governments, on a cost-reimbursement basis.

Investment trust fund – A generic fund type within the fiduciary category used by a government in a fiduciary capacity, such as to maintain its cash and investment pool for other governments.

Major funds – A government's general fund (or its equivalent), other individual governmental type, and enterprise funds that meet specific quantitative criteria, and any other governmental or enterprise fund that a government's officials believe is particularly important to financial statement users.

Management's discussion and analysis – Management's discussion and analysis, or MD&A, is required supplementary information that introduces the basic financial statements by presenting certain financial information as well as management's analytical insights on that information.

Measurement focus – The accounting convention that determines (a) which assets and which liabilities are included on a government's balance sheet and where they are reported, and (b) whether an operating statement presents information on the flow of financial resources (revenues and expenditures) or information on the flow of economic resources (revenues and expenses).

Modified accrual basis of accounting – The basis of accounting adapted to the governmental fund type measurement focus. Revenues and other financial resource increments are recognized when they become both *measurable* and *available to finance expenditures of the current period. Available* means collectible in the current period or soon enough thereafter to be used to pay liabilities of the current period. Expenditures are recognized when the fund liability is incurred and expected to be paid from current resources, except for (a) inventories of materials and supplies that may be considered expenditures either when purchased or when used and (b) prepaid insurance and similar items that may be considered expenditures either when paid for or when consumed. All governmental funds are accounted for using the modified accrual basis of accounting in fund financial statements.

Modified approach – Rules that allow infrastructure assets that are part of a network or subsystem of a network not to be depreciated as long as certain requirements are met.

Net Position – the residual of all other elements presented in a statement of financial position.

Nonspendable fund balance – The portion of fund balance that includes amounts that cannot be spent because they are either (a) not in spendable form or (b) legally or contractually required to be maintained intact.

Pension trust fund – A trust fund used to account for a public employees retirement system. Pension trust funds use the accrual basis of accounting and the flow of economic resources measurement focus.

Permanent fund – A generic fund type under the governmental category used to report resources that are legally restricted to the extent that only earnings, and not principal, may be used for purposes that support the reporting government's programs and, therefore, are for the benefit of the government or its citizenry. (Permanent funds do not include private-purpose trust funds, which should be used when the government is required to use the principal or earnings for the benefit of individuals, private organizations, or other governments).

Private purpose trust fund – A general fund type under the fiduciary category used to report resources held and administered by the reporting government acting in a fiduciary capacity for individuals, other governments, or private organizations.

Proprietary funds – The government category used to account for a government's ongoing organizations and activities that are similar to those often found in the private sector (these are enterprise and internal service funds). All assets, liabilities, equities, revenues, expenses, and transfers relating to the government's business and quasi-business activities are accounted for through proprietary funds. Proprietary funds should apply all applicable GASB pronouncements and those GAAP applicable to similar businesses in the private sector, unless those conflict with GASB pronouncements. These funds use the accrual basis of accounting in conjunction with the flow of economic resources measurement focus.

Purchases method – The method under which inventories are recorded as expenditures when acquired.

Restricted fund balance – Portion of fund balance that reflects constraints placed on the use of resources (other than non-spendable items) that are either (a) externally imposed by a creditor, such as through debt covenants, grantors, contributors, or laws or regulations of other governments or (b) imposed by law through constitutional provisions or enabling legislation.

Required supplementary information – GAAP specify that certain information be presented as required supplementary information, or RSI.

Special-purpose governments –Legally separate entities that perform only one activity or a few activities, such as cemetery districts, school districts, colleges and universities, utilities, hospitals and other health care organizations, and public employee retirement systems.

Special revenue fund – A fund that *must* have revenue or proceeds from specific revenue sources that are either restricted or committed for a specific purpose other than debt service or capital projects. This definition means that in order to be considered a special revenue fund, there must be one or more revenue sources upon which reporting the activity in a separate fund is predicated.

Interfund Transfers – All transfers, such as legally authorized transfers from a fund receiving revenue to a fund through which the resources are to be expended, where there is no intent to repay. Interfund transfers are recorded on the operating statement.

Unassigned fund balance – Residual classification for the general fund. This classification represents fund balance that has not been assigned to other funds and has not been restricted, committed, or assigned to specific purposes within the general fund. The general fund should be the only fund that reports a positive unassigned fund balance amount. In other funds, if expenditures incurred for specific purposes exceeded the amounts restricted, committed, or assigned to those purposes, it may be necessary to report a negative unassigned fund balance.

Unrestricted fund balance – The total of committed fund balance, assigned fund balance, and unassigned fund balance.

Not-for-Profit terminology

Board-designated endowment fund – An endowment fund created by a not-for-profit entity's governing board by designating a portion of its net assets without donor restrictions to be invested to provide income for a long, but not necessarily specified, period.

Board-designated net assets – Net assets without donor restrictions subject to self-imposed limits by action of the governing board. Board-designated net assets may be earmarked for future programs, investment, contingencies, purchase or construction of fixed assets, or other uses.

Charitable lead trust – A trust established in connection with a split-interest agreement in which the not-for-profit entity receives distributions during the agreement's term. Upon termination of the trust, the remainder of the trust assets is paid to the donor or to third-party beneficiaries designated by the donor.

Charitable remainder trust – A trust established in connection with a split-interest agreement in which the donor or a third-party beneficiary receives specified distributions during the agreement's term. Upon termination of the trust, a not-for-profit entity receives the assets remaining in the trust.

Collections – Works of art, historical treasures, or similar assets that are (a) held for public exhibition, education, or research in furtherance of public service, rather than financial gain, (b) protected, kept unencumbered, cared for, and preserved, and (c) subject to an organizational policy that requires the proceeds of items that are sold to be used to acquire other items for collections.

Conditional promise to give – A promise to give that depends on the occurrence of a specified future and uncertain event to bind the promisor.

Contribution – An unconditional transfer of cash or other assets to an entity or a settlement or cancellation of its liabilities in a voluntary nonreciprocal transfer by another entity acting other than as an owner.

Costs of joint activities –Costs incurred for a joint activity. Costs of joint activities may include joint costs and costs other than joint costs. *Costs other than joint costs* are costs that are identifiable with a particular function, such as program, fundraising, management and general, and membership development costs.

Donor-imposed restriction – A donor stipulation (*donors* include other types of contributors, including makers of certain grants) that specifies a use for the contributed asset that is more specific than broad limits resulting from the nature of the organization, the environment in which it operates, and the purposes specified in its articles of incorporation or bylaws, or comparable documents for an unincorporated association. A restriction on an organization's use of the asset contributed may be temporary in nature or perpetual in nature.

Donor-restricted endowment fund – An endowment fund that is created by a donor stipulation (*donors* include other types of contributors, including makers of certain grants) that requires investment of the gift in perpetuity or for a specified term. Some donors or laws may require that a portion of income, gains, or both be added to the gift and invested subject to similar restrictions.

Donor-restricted support – Donor-restricted revenues or gains from contributions that increase net assets with donor restrictions (*donors* include other types of contributions, including makers of certain grants).

Economic interest – A not-for-profit entity's interest in another entity that exists if any of the following criteria are met: (a) The other entity holds or uses significant resources that must be used for the purposes of the not-for-profit entity, either directly or indirectly, by producing income or providing services, or (b) the not-for-profit entity is responsible for the liabilities of the other entity.

Endowment fund – An established fund of cash, securities, or other assets that provides income for the maintenance of a not-for-profit entity. The use of the assets of the fund may be with or without donor-imposed restrictions. Endowment funds generally are established by donor-restricted gifts and bequests to provide a source of income in perpetuity or for a specified period.

Functional expense classification – A method of grouping expenses according to the purpose for which the costs are incurred. The primary functional classifications of a not-for-profit entity are program services and supporting activities.

Funds functioning as endowment – Net assets without donor restrictions (*donors* include other types of contributors, including makers of certain grants) designated by an entity's governing board to be invested to provide income for generally a long, but not necessarily specified, period.

Joint activity – An activity that is part of the fundraising function and has elements of one or more other functions, such as programs, management and general, membership development, or any other functional category used by the entity.

Joint costs – The costs of conducting joint activities that are not identifiable with a particular component of the activity.

Management and general activities – Supporting activities that are not directly identifiable with one or more programs, fundraising activities, or membership development activities.

Natural expense classification – A method of grouping expenses according to the kinds of economic benefits received in incurring those expenses. Examples of natural expense classifications include salaries and wages, employee benefits, professional services, supplies, interest expense, rent, utilities, and depreciation.

Net assets – The excess or deficiency of assets over liabilities of a not-for-profit entity, which is divided into two mutually exclusive classes according to the existence or absence of donor-imposed restrictions.

Net assets with donor restrictions – The part of net assets of a not-for-profit entity that is subject to donor-imposed restrictions (*donors* include other types of contributors, including makers of certain grants).

Net assets without donor restrictions – The part of net assets of a not-for-profit entity that is not subject to donor-imposed restrictions (*donors* include other types of contributors, including makers of certain grants).

Permanently restricted net assets – The part of the net assets of a not-for-profit organization resulting from (a) contributions and other inflows of assets whose use by the organization is limited by donor-imposed stipulations that neither expire by passage of time nor can be fulfilled or otherwise removed by actions of the organization, (b) other asset enhancements and diminishments subject to the same kinds of stipulations, and (c) reclassifications from (or to) other classes of net assets as a consequence of donor-imposed stipulations. Will be superseded upon implementation of FASB Accounting Standards Update (ASU) No. 2016-14, *Not-for-Profit Entities (Topic 958): Presentation of Financial Statements of Not-for-Profit Entities.*

Programmatic investing – The activity of making loans or other investments that are directed at carrying out a not-for-profit entity's purpose for existence, rather than investing in the general production of income or appreciation of an asset (for example, total return investing). An example of programmatic investing is a loan made to lower-income individuals to promote home ownership.

Promise to give – A written or oral agreement to contribute cash or other assets to another entity. A promise to give may be either conditional or unconditional.

Underwater endowment fund – A donor-restricted endowment fund for which the fair value of the fund at the reporting date is less than either the original gift amount or the amount required to be maintained by the donor or by law that extends donor restrictions.

Temporarily restricted net assets – The part of the net assets of a not-for-profit entity resulting from (a) contributions and other inflows of assets whose use by the organization is limited by donor-imposed stipulations that either expire by the passage of time or can be fulfilled and removed by actions of the entity pursuant to those stipulations, (b) other asset enhancements and diminishments subject to the same kinds of stipulations, and (c) reclassifications to (or from) other classes of net assets as a consequence of donor-imposed stipulations, their expiration by passage of time, or their fulfillment and removal by actions of the entity pursuant to those stipulations. Will be superseded upon implementation of ASU No. 2016-14.

Unrestricted net assets – The part of net assets of a not-for-profit entity that is neither permanently restricted nor temporarily restricted by donor-imposed stipulations. Will be superseded upon implementation of ASU No. 2016-14.

Single audit and yellow book terminology

Attestation engagements – Attestation engagements concern examining, reviewing, or performing agreed-upon procedures on a subject matter or an assertion about a subject matter and reporting on the results.

Compliance supplement – A document issued annually in the spring by the OMB to provide guidance to auditors.

Data collection form – A form submitted to the Federal Audit Clearinghouse that provides information about the auditor, the auditee and its federal programs, and the results of the audit.

Federal financial assistance – Assistance that nonfederal entities receive or administer in the form of grants, loans, loan guarantees, property, cooperative agreements, interest subsidies, insurance, food commodities, direct appropriations, or other assistance, but does not include amounts received as reimbursement for services rendered to individuals in accordance with guidance issued by the Director.

Financial audits – Financial audits are primarily concerned with providing reasonable assurance about whether financial statements are presented fairly, in all material respects, in conformity with GAAP or with a comprehensive basis of accounting other than GAAP.

GAGAS – Generally accepted government auditing standards issued by the GAO. They are also commonly known as the Yellow Book.

GAO – The United States Government Accountability Office. Among its responsibilities is the issuance of GAGAS (that is, the Yellow Book).

OMB – The Office of Management and Budget. The OMB assists the President in the development and implementation of budget, program, management, and regulatory policies.

Pass-through entity – A nonfederal entity that provides federal awards to a subrecipient to carry out a federal program.

Performance audits – Performance audits entail an objective and systematic examination of evidence to provide an independent assessment of the performance and management of a program against objective criteria as well as assessments that provide a prospective focus or that synthesize information on best practices or cross-cutting issues.

Program-specific audit – A compliance audit of one federal program.

Single audit – An audit of a nonfederal entity that includes the entity's financial statements and federal awards.

Single Audit Guide – This AICPA Audit Guide, formally titled Government Auditing Standards *and Single Audits* (the Single Audit Guide), is the former Statement of Position (SOP) 98-3. The Single Audit Guide provides guidance on the auditor's responsibilities when conducting a single audit or program-specific audit in accordance with the Single Audit Act, GAGAS, and the Uniform Guidance.

Subrecipient – A nonfederal entity that receives federal awards through another nonfederal entity to carry out a federal program but does not include an individual who receives financial assistance through such awards.

Uniform Guidance – Title 2 U.S. *Code of Federal Regulations* Part 200, *Uniform Administrative Requirements, Cost Principles, and Audit Requirements for Federal Awards* (Uniform Guidance), sets forth the requirements for the compliance audit portion of a single audit.

Index

W

NOT-FOR-PROFIT FINANCIAL REPORTING: MASTERING THE UNIQUE REQUIREMENTS

BY BRUCE W. CHASE, PH.D., CPA

Solutions

The AICPA publishes *CPA Letter Daily*, a free e-newsletter published each weekday. The newsletter, which covers the 10-12 most important stories in business, finance, and accounting, as well as AICPA information, was created to deliver news to CPAs and others who work with the accounting profession. Besides summarizing media articles, commentaries, and research results, the e-newsletter links to television broadcasts and videos and features reader polls. *CPA Letter Daily*'s editors scan hundreds of publications and websites, selecting the most relevant and important news so you don't have to. The newsletter arrives in your inbox early in the morning. To sign up, visit smartbrief.com/CPA.

Do you need high-quality technical assistance? The AICPA Auditing and Accounting Technical Hotline provides non-authoritative guidance on accounting, auditing, attestation, and compilation and review standards. The hotline can be reached at 877.242.7212.

Solutions

Chapter 1

Case study solutions

There are several deficiencies in the statement prepared by Bob, including the following:

- The statement would report only two classes of net assets: net assets without donor restrictions and net assets with donor restrictions.
- The statement does not report a change in total net assets for the year.
- The statement reports the using up of restricted resources as expenses in net assets with donor restrictions. All expenses should be recorded as decreases in net assets without donor restrictions. Using resources to meet a donor-stipulated restriction would decrease net assets with donor restrictions and increase net assets without donor restrictions simultaneously.
- It appears that all gifts were recorded as increases in net assets without donor restrictions and the restricted gifts then transferred to the proper class of net assets. Restricted gifts should be recorded directly in the proper class of net assets.
- The statement uses the term expenditures instead of expenses. The statement should report expenses, not expenditures.
- The statement reports depreciation. This is not a functional classification of expense.

The following are additional observations about Bob's statement. They are not errors.

- The statement is titled "statement of operations," not the statement of activities. It is acceptable to label this statement something other than the statement of activities.
- The statement reports a "loss from operations." This is acceptable. An entity may choose to report some intermediate measure of operations, such as operating revenues over expenses.
- The statement does not report total revenue or expenses. Revenues, gains, expenses, losses, and reclassifications can be arranged in a variety of orders. There is no requirement to report totals for these items.

The following are possible additional changes from the implementation of FASB ASU 2016-14:

- Additional information would need to be disclosed in the footnotes for any board designations on net assets without donor restrictions.
- The entity would also be required to present expenses by function and nature in one location.
- The NFP would be required to disclose both quantitative and qualitative information about liquidity of assets and short-term demands on those assets.

Practice question solutions

1. c.
2. c.
3. d.
4. c.
5. a.
6. d.
7. d.

Knowledge check solutions

1.

a. Correct. Footnote disclosures are required to include the timing and nature of the donor-imposed restrictions, as well as the composition of net assets with donor restrictions at the end of the period. The disclosures will continue to show an analysis by time, purpose, and perpetual restrictions.

b. Incorrect. Management cannot impose such restrictions; board designations would be classified as net assets without donor restrictions.

c. Incorrect. Without donor-imposed restrictions, net assets are classified as net assets without donor restrictions.

d. Incorrect. Endowment funds with donor-imposed restrictions do not expire with the passage of time.

2.

a. Incorrect. In general, FASB ASC 958 allows significant flexibility in presenting certain information, allowing financial reporting to evolve to meet the needs of different NFP groups.

b. Correct. FASB ASC 958 focuses on reporting aggregated information about the entity as a whole.

c. Incorrect. The general purpose financial statements required by FASB ASC 958 for NFP entities are the statement of financial position, the statement of activities, the statement of cash flows, and accompanying notes to the financial statements. The statement of functional expense is not a required statement; however the information is required to be disclosed either on the face of the statement of activities, in the notes, or as a separate statement.

d. Incorrect. FASB ASC 958 does not require information be reported by funds.

3.

    a. Correct. In many ways, the statement of activities is like an income statement for an NFP organization.

    b. Incorrect. Because NFP entities have an operating purpose other than making a profit, terms like income statement and net income are not used.

    c. Incorrect. The statement of activities focuses on the entity as a whole.

    d. Incorrect. Entities are not required to report some intermediate measure of operations, such as operating revenues over expenses.

4.

    a. Correct. The statement of activities reports revenues, gains, expenses, and losses for the period.

    b. Incorrect. Revenues are reported as increases in net assets without donor restrictions unless the use of the assets received is limited by donor-imposed restrictions.

    c. Incorrect. All expenses are reported as decreases in net assets without donor restrictions.

    d. Incorrect. NFP entities have much flexibility in how items are sequenced in the statement of activities.

5.

    a. Correct. Investments that are purchased are recorded at their acquisition costs.

    b. Incorrect. Investments that are contributed are recorded at fair value.

    c. Incorrect. Derivative instruments are measured at fair value.

    d. Incorrect. Not all investments are recorded at cost.

6.

    a. Incorrect. Investment income includes dividends.

    b. Incorrect. If there are no donor-imposed restrictions on the use of the income, it should be reported as an increase in net assets without donor restrictions.

    c. Correct. Investment income includes interest.

    d. Incorrect. Investment income includes gains on investments.

7.

a. Correct. Realized gains and losses arise from selling or otherwise disposing of investments.

b. Incorrect. If realized gains and losses arise from selling or otherwise disposing of investments for which unrealized gains and losses have been recognized in the statement of activities of prior reporting periods, the amount reported in the statement of activities as gains or losses upon the sale or other disposition of the investments should exclude the amount that has previously been recognized in the statement of activities.

c. Incorrect. Realized gains and losses should be reported in the statement of activities as changes in net assets without donor restrictions unless their use is restricted by explicit donor-imposed stipulations or by law.

d. Incorrect. Unrealized gain and losses on investments reported at fair value are reported in the statement of activities.

Chapter 2

Case study solutions

Item	Should the contributed service be recognized? If the service should be recognized, how might you value the service?
The normal duties of the treasurer	The HSNRV should not record contributed services for the normal duties of the treasurer. Although the current treasurer is a CPA and has specialized skills, the signing of checks and review of reconciliations does not require such skills and the entity would not normally purchase such services if they had not been contributed.
The football coach's speech	The HSNRV would probably not record contributed services for the football coach's speech. It is assumed that the entity would not normally purchase such services if they had not been contributed. However, if they would purchase this service, it would be recorded and valued at the speaker's normal rate. The speaker has specialized skills required for a kickoff event.

Review the questions listed in the following chart related to HSNRV. Use the right column to answer each question.

Question	Answer
How would you prepare the journal entry for the 200 people who pledged $100 each to be paid within 1 year?	Based on past experience, the college expects to collect 95% of this amount. Contributions arising from unconditional promises to give that are expected to be collected within one year may be measured at their net realizable value. The entry would be as follows: dr. Contributions Receivable $19,000 cr. Contribution Revenue — increase in net assets with donor restrictions $19,000 (**Note:** Some NFPs may use a subsidiary ledger to retain information concerning the $20,000 face amount of contributions promised in order to monitor collections of contributions promised.)

Question	Answer
How would you prepare the journal entry for the 20 people who pledged $10,000 each to be paid in 3 years?	The college expects to collect 90% of this amount. The college estimates the present value to be $155,000. The entry would be as follows: dr. Contributions Receivable $180,000 cr. Contribution Revenue — Increase in net assets with donor restrictions $155,000 cr. Discount on Contributions Receivable $25,000 (**Note:** Similar to the preceding answer, some NFPs may use a subsidiary ledger to retain information concerning the $200,000 face amount of contributions promised in order to monitor collections of contributions promised.)

How should the following transactions be reported? (unconditional contribution, conditional contribution, exchange transaction) Also indicate if the transaction would increase net assets with donor restrictions. Use the right column to answer each question.

Item	Answer
Donor A contribute $5,000 to purchase new beds for the shelter	This is an unconditional contribution that would increase net assets with donor restrictions.
The HSNRV receives a federal grant of $50,000 to support housing 10 homeless people.	This is an unconditional contribution that increase net assets without donor restriction. The grant is for societal benefit does not represent commensurate value. The terms of this grant are in line with the organization's mission, which is why it's considered net assets without donor restrictions.
Donor B promises to contribute $10,000 if the HSNRV increases the number of people served by the shelter by 10% in the coming year	This is conditional promise to give based on a barrier. It would not be reported until the conditions are substantially
The local hardware store enters into an agreement with HSNRV to pay $10 per straw baskets made by people staying at the shelter. The fair value of the baskets is $6.	This transaction would be part exchange and part contribution. The fair value of the baskets would be the exchange amount and the difference would be a contribution.

Practice question solutions

1. d.
2. a.
3. a.
4. c.
5. RC Unconditional promises to give with payments due in future periods

   UC Gift of a car the entity plans to sell

   E Dues that cover the cost of publications

   RC Gift of securities to create an endowment fund

   NR Gift of art work to a collection (collection not capitalized)

   UC Donated accounting services by a CPA

   UC Free use of office space in the current year

   NR Conditional promise to give if an organization can raise a certain amount

   UC Donated services to replace a roof

Knowledge check solutions

1.
   a. Correct. NFPs receive resources from activities such as investment activities.
   b. Incorrect. NFP entities receive inflows of resources from a variety of sources.
   c. Incorrect. Inflows from transfers where the entity is acting as an agent, trustee, or other intermediary for the donor are referred to as agency transactions.
   d. Incorrect. NFPs do engage in reciprocal (exchange) transactions.

2.
   a. Correct. Exchange transaction revenues result from an entity satisfying a performance obligation by transferring a promised good or service to a customer.
   b. Incorrect. Fees charged for providing goods and services to members, clients, students, and customers that receive substantive benefits are revenues from exchange transactions.
   c. Incorrect. In some situations, judgment is required to determine whether an increase in net assets should be reported as a revenue or as a gain.
   d. Incorrect. A transaction can be considered part exchange and part contribution.

3.

   a. Correct. Revenues from exchange transactions should be recognized based on accrual accounting principles.

   b. Incorrect. The recognition, measurement, and display of revenues and related receivables arising from exchange transactions are similar for both NFP and for-profit entities.

   c. Incorrect. Revenues from exchange transactions should be reported as increases in unrestricted net assets in a statement of activities.

   d. Incorrect. Revenue should be reported net of regularly provided discounts.

4.

   a. Correct. Some entities receive grants, awards, or sponsorships from other entities. Many of these are contributions, but some of these items may be exchange transactions.

   b. Incorrect. If dues are classified as exchange transactions, they should be recognized as revenue as the earnings process is completed.

   c. Incorrect. Some entities receive dues from their members. These dues may be considered exchange, part exchange and part contribution, or all contribution.

   d. Incorrect. If items of nominal value are given, the transaction will still be reported as a contribution.

5.

   a. Correct. A conditional promise to give should be recognized only when the conditions are substantially met.

   b. Incorrect. An example of a conditional contribution is where a donor pledges $100,000 if the entity can raise an additional $100,000 in the next 12 months.

   c. Incorrect. Donor-imposed conditions should be substantially met by the entity before the receipt of assets (including contributions receivable) is recognized as a contribution.

   d. Incorrect. Conditional promises to give can contain restrictions.

6.

   a. Correct. Donor-imposed restrictions can either be purpose, time or perpetual in nature.

   b. Incorrect. In some cases, donor-imposed restrictions are met in the same period that the contribution is received.

   c. Incorrect. Generally, restrictions are stipulated explicitly by the donor in a written or oral communication accompanying the gift.

   d. Incorrect. Contributions can have implied restrictions.

7.

    a. Correct. Examples of activities that may be reported as gains and losses would include changes in fair value of equity securities.

    b. Incorrect. An important determination in financial reporting for NFPs is whether an item is a revenue or expense, or a gain or loss.

    c. Incorrect. Donations received at an annual fund-raising event would be considered revenue.

    d. Incorrect. Gains and losses can be reported for all classes of net assets.

Chapter 3

Case study solutions

How should the following expenses be reported by functional classification (program activities, management and general activities, or fund-raising activities)? Use the right column to answer each question.	
Expense	Answer
Catering and entertainment for the special fund-raising event cost $15,000	Supporting activities that can be reported as part of management and general activities or as costs of direct benefit to others. This is an annual event and expenses are reported gross.
Promotional costs of $5,000for the special fund-raising event	Fund-raising activities
President's salary $45,000 (president spent 40% of her time counseling people in the shelter)	Program services $18,000, Management and general activities $27,000 Some expenses relate to more than one program or supporting activity and must be allocated to the appropriate functions.
Shelter workers $40,000 (cleaning and preparing meals)	Program services Program services are activities that result in goods and services being distributed to beneficiaries, customers, or members that fulfill the purposes or mission of the organization
Shelter utilizes and supplies $15,000	Program services
Bookkeeper $10,000	Management and general activities
Annual audit fee and report $4,000	Management and general activities
Annual fund-raising letters $5,000	Fund-raising activities

Practice question solutions

1. a.
2. c.
3. b.

Knowledge check solutions

1.
 a. Incorrect. Program services are activities that result in goods and services being distributed to beneficiaries, customers, or members that fulfill the purposes or mission of the organization.
 b. Incorrect. Supporting services may include, as one or more separate categories, cost of sales and costs of other revenue-generating activities that are not program related.
 c. Correct. Supporting services are activities other than program services and include management and general, fund-raising, and membership-development activities.
 d. Incorrect. Classification of supporting services other than management and general and fund-raising can be used by entities.

2.
 a. Correct. The proper classification of expenses between program services and supporting services is often important to NFP entities.
 b. Incorrect. An entity must report expense information about program services that it provides.
 c. Incorrect. Resource providers often compare the percentage of expenses that go to providing program services to the percentage of expenses that go to supporting services.
 d. Incorrect. Functional reporting of expenses can be reported in the statement of activities or in the notes to the financial statements.

3.
 a. Incorrect. One entity may report a single classification of program expenses, while others may report several classifications.
 b. Incorrect. Entities may consider guidance in FASB ASC 280 in determining the number of major classes to use.
 c. Correct. The number of classes to use requires professional judgment.
 d. Incorrect. There is no limit on the number of program service classifications.

4.

    a. Incorrect. They include budgeting activities.

    b. Incorrect. They include oversight activities.

    c. Correct. They include financing activities.

    d. Incorrect. They exclude fund-raising.

5.

    a. Correct: The analysis is required for all NFP entities.

    b. Incorrect: The analysis reports expenses by functional and natural classification.

    c. Incorrect: It is required for all NFP entities.

    d. Incorrect: The analysis is required for all NFP entities.

Chapter 4

Case study solution part 1

Case study

Case study solution for exercise 1

Ratio	Answer
Liquidity	Current assets / current liabilities $25,000 / $10,000 = 1.25
Operating strength	Net assets without donor restrictions / operating expenses $60,000 / $100,000 = .6
Debt ratio	Debt / total assets $15,000 / $75,000 = .2
Program effectiveness	Program expense / total expenses $70,000 / $100,000 = .7
Fund-raising efficiency	Fund-raising expense / contributions $10,000 / $100,000 = .1

Case study (continued)

Case study solution for exercise 2

Items	Answer
Cost per meal served	Efficiency measure
Number of meals served	Output measure
Hours spent preparing the meals	Input measure
Number of malnutrition cases reported	Outcome measure over time
Amount spent on food	Input measure
Number of people served	Output measure

Practice question solutions

1. d.
2. a.
3. d.
4. d.
5. c.
6. c.
7. a.
8. b.

Knowledge check solutions

1.
    a. Correct. Many of the services NFP entities provide do not have a direct relationship to how much the recipient pays.
    b. Incorrect. There are several accounting and reporting issues related to contributions.
    c. Incorrect. Many NFP entities depend on donations as a major source of their operational funding.
    d. Incorrect. NFP entities do enter into many of the same transactions as businesses.

2.

    a. Correct. Differences in the environment factors result in NFP entities having unique financial reporting objectives.

    b. Incorrect. NFP reporting objectives are different from those of a business.

    c. Incorrect. NFP entities should provide information that is useful to present and future resource providers in making rational decisions about the allocation of resources to those entities.

    d. Incorrect. Profitability is not a key reporting objective of NFP entities.

3.

    a. Incorrect. NFP entities should provide information that is useful to present and future resource providers in assessing the services that the entity provides and its ability to continue to provide those services.

    b. Incorrect. Determining profitability and net income are not part of the objectives for NFP entities.

    c. Correct. NFP entities should provide information that is useful to present and future resource providers in assessing how managers have discharged their stewardship responsibilities and other aspects of their performance.

    d. Incorrect. Unique accounting and reporting practices are needed by NFP entities to meet financial reporting objectives.

4.

    a. Correct. Some NFP entities include fund information in their external financial reports.

    b. Incorrect. The financial statements presented by NFPs are not based on fund accounting but on external restrictions.

    c. Incorrect. Many NFP entities use fund accounting for internal recordkeeping purposes.

    d. Incorrect. NFP entities report two classes of net assets.

5.

    a. Correct. Many stakeholders are interested in the financial performance of NFP entities.

    b. Incorrect. There is limited value in saying that items such as cash, net assets, or certain revenues or expenses are of some amount.

    c. Incorrect. Financial statements contain a lot of numbers and can be difficult to analyze.

    d. Incorrect. Trend analysis is a tool that can be used to measure financial performance.

6.

    a. Correct. Comparing the financial statements among different NFP entities can have limited value because entities can vary greatly in size and scope, making direct dollar value comparisons difficult.

    b. Incorrect. Common size statements are a tool that can be used.

    c. Incorrect. There are tools that can be used to bring more meaning to the numbers presented on financial statements.

    d. Incorrect. There is a ratio to measure fund-raising efficiency.

7.

    a. Correct. There are several ways to judge the performance of an NFP organization.

    b. Incorrect. Just spending resources on providing a service is not an effective measure of performance.

    c. Incorrect. For most entities, a higher percentage of resources spent on program services is considered a positive performance indicator.

    d. Incorrect. FASB recognizes the limitations of traditional financial statements for assessing performance of NFP entities.

8.

    a. Correct. Outcome measures are a category of service efforts and accomplishment measures.

    b. Incorrect. In FASB Concepts Statement No. 4, the need for a different type of information to measure the performance of NFP entities is identified.

    c. Incorrect. Efficiency measures are a category of service efforts and accomplishment measures.

    d. Incorrect. Input measures are used to report the level of effort expended.

The AICPA publishes *CPA Letter Daily*, a free e-newsletter published each weekday. The newsletter, which covers the 10-12 most important stories in business, finance, and accounting, as well as AICPA information, was created to deliver news to CPAs and others who work with the accounting profession. Besides summarizing media articles, commentaries, and research results, the e-newsletter links to television broadcasts and videos and features reader polls. *CPA Letter Daily*'s editors scan hundreds of publications and websites, selecting the most relevant and important news so you don't have to. The newsletter arrives in your inbox early in the morning. To sign up, visit smartbrief.com/CPA.

Do you need high-quality technical assistance? The AICPA Auditing and Accounting Technical Hotline provides non-authoritative guidance on accounting, auditing, attestation, and compilation and review standards. The hotline can be reached at 877.242.7212.

Learn More

Continuing Professional Education

Thank you for selecting the American Institute of Certified Public Accountants as your continuing professional education provider. We have a diverse offering of CPE courses to help you expand your skillset and develop your competencies. Choose from hundreds of different titles spanning the major subject matter areas relevant to CPAs and CGMAs, including:

- Governmental and not-for-profit accounting, auditing, and updates
- Internal control and fraud
- Audits of employee benefit plans and 401(k) plans
- Individual and corporate tax updates
- A vast array of courses in other areas of accounting and auditing, controllership, management, consulting, taxation, and more!

Get your CPE when and where you want

- Self-study training options that includes on-demand, webcasts, and text formats with superior quality and a broad portfolio of topics, including bundled products like –
  - ➤ CPExpress® online learning for immediate access to hundreds of one- to four-credit hour online courses for just-in-time learning at a price that is right
  - ➤ Annual Webcast Pass offering live Q&A with experts and unlimited access to the scheduled lineup, all at an incredible discount.
- Staff training programs for audit, tax and preparation, compilation, and review
- Certificate programs offering comprehensive curriculums developed by practicing experts to build fundamental core competencies in specialized topics
- National conferences presented by recognized experts
- Affordable courses on-site at your organization – visit **aicpalearning.org/on-site** for more information.
- Seminars sponsored by your state society and led by top instructors. For a complete list, visit **aicpalearning.org/publicseminar**.

Take control of your career development

The AICPA's Competency and Learning website at **https://competency.aicpa.org** brings together a variety of learning resources and a self-assessment tool, enabling tracking and reporting of progress toward learning goals.

Visit **www.AICPAStore.com** to browse our CPE selections.

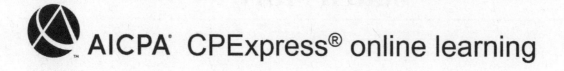

AICPA® CPExpress® online learning

Just-in-time learning at your fingertips 24/7

Where can you get <u>unlimited online access</u> to 600+ credit hours (450+ CPE courses) for one low annual subscription fee?

CPExpress® online learning, the AICPA's comprehensive bundle of online continuing professional education courses for CPAs, offers you immediate access to hundreds of one- to four-credit hour courses. You can choose from a full spectrum of subject areas and knowledge levels to select the specific topic you need when you need it for just-in-time learning.
Access hundreds of courses for one low annual subscription price!

How can CPExpress® online learning help you?

- ✓ Start and finish most CPE courses in as little as 1 to 2 hours with 24/7 access so you can fit CPE into a busy schedule.

- ✓ Quickly brush up or get a brief overview on hundreds of topics when you need it.

- ✓ Create and customize your personal online course catalog for quick access with hot topics at your fingertips.

- ✓ Print CPE certificates on demand to document your training – never miss a CPE reporting deadline.

Quantity Purchases for Firm or Corporate Accounts
If you have 5 or more employees who require training, the firm access option allows you to purchase multiple seats. Plus, you can designate an administrator who will be able to monitor the training progress of each staff member. To learn more about firm access and group pricing, visit aicpalearning.org/cpexpress or call 800.634.6780.

To subscribe, visit www.AICPAStore.com/cpexpress

Your strategic learning partner
Let us help prepare your staff for the future.

What is your current approach to learning? One size does not fit all. Your organization is unique, and your approach to learning and competency should be, too. But where do you start? Choose a strategic partner to help you assess competencies and gaps, design a customized learning plan, and measure and maximize the ROI of your learning and development initiatives.

We offer a wide variety of learning programs for finance professionals at every stage of their career.

AICPA Learning resources can help you:
- Create a learning culture to attract and retain talent
- Enrich staff competency and stay current on changing regulations
- Sharpen your competitive edge
- Capitalize on emerging opportunities
- Meet your goals and positively impact your bottom line
- Address CPE/CPD compliance

Flexible learning options include:
- On-site training
- Conferences
- Webcasts
- Certificate programs
- Online self-study
- Publications

An investment in learning can directly impact your bottom line. Contact an AICPA learning consultant to begin your professional development planning.

Call: 800.634.6780, option 1
Email: AICPALearning@aicpa.org